IT'S GETTING GOODER

AND GOODER

IT'S GETTING GOODER
AND GOODER

by

HYMIE RUBENSTEIN

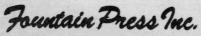

BOX 7
HARRISON, ARKANSAS 72601

International Standard Book Number: 0-89350-006-2

DEDICATION

TO:

My wife, Elaine, and my three daughters, Leilah-Ann, Laina-Jane, and Lilly.

And to my friends:

Huss Water and Joan: for their faithfulness in helping me compile the book.

United Airways: where most of the book was prepared— "In the friendly skies."

Demos Shakarian: (President, FGBMFI) for his power of perseverance which greatly encouraged me.

Simon Vikse: (FGBMFI, director) for his blessed wisdom which I admired and copied.

FOREWORD

It was an early Saturday morning at the American Hotel in New York City that I first met Hymie Rubenstein. He was to be the speaker for the Full Gospel Business Men's breakfast that morning.

Since then, he has been speaking in three of our New York Regional Conventions. As convention chairman and one of the FGBMFI international directors, I have greatly appreciated Hymie's ministry. He has been a blessing to many people in our city. He has a unique way of presenting his testimony, with an added touch of humor that holds his audience spellbound.

Hymie came with us on the Scandinavian Airlift, and joined our team to Norway. He spoke in many of the meetings as we traveled around that country. One meeting was held in the Lutheran Church in the picturesque city of Bergen. Many people were ministered to and we were invited by the minister to come back. Hymie's testimony of how God saved him has been a great encouragement to many all over the world, and I know as you read this book you will be blessed also.

Simon Vikse

CONTENTS

PREFACE

This is a book about a Jewish man who was so enveloped in materialistic things that he had no time to consider or contemplate the possibility of allowing God to occupy His rightful place in his life.

Blinded by greed and the lust for riches and power, he failed to see that the good things of life are free. Suddenly destruction stared him in the face, and there was no way to escape.

Most unexpectedly God undertook for him through His only begotten Son Christ Jesus, and raised a standard against the devil who would destroy him. The reality becomes so very real that he immediately decides that he is not ashamed of the Gospel of Christ Jesus, knowing that it is the only way to salvation to *whosoever* would believe. . . first to the Jew, then the Greek, and the whole wide world.

This Jewish man does something about it. He travels from city to city, from state to state, from country to country advertising "The Lamb of God who heals body, mind and spirit, and takes away the sins of the world."

As author of this book it is my desire to be a blessing to the discouraged, a comfort to the fearful, and a help to the needy (physically, spiritually, mentally and financially).

Above all, I pray that many might come to the realization that Almighty God is good, kind, forgiving and understanding. That He is the great creator of mankind. The great architect of the world, and the great geometrician of the universe.

May the reader of this book experience a personal relationship with God the Father, God the Son and God the Holy Ghost.

We serve a High Priest that can be touched with the feelings of our infirmities (Hebrews 4:15).

To my Jewish readers I say, *Shalom.*

—H. R.

Chapter One
A Jewish Youth in South Africa

Life was so wonderful. So fascinating. So very thrilling. I was possibly the happiest Jewish boy in the junior school, or in the whole wide world. I was boxing champion in my division. I was captain of my Rugby (football) Team, and the class had voted me most popular boy of the year. The teacher had asked me to carry her bags home for her after school. She promised that I could do this for a whole week. The smile she gave me with the promise just set my heart afire. This was one of the greatest honors that could be bestowed upon any boy or girl in the class. Then one day when she announced to the class that I was her "Knight Errant" I loved her more than ever. If that was possible.

I was always taller than most of the boys my age, and I always took exceptional care to be extra clean and tidy at all times. My sneakers were always of the whitest. The crease on my blue shorts were practically razor sharp. My white shirt and bright-red tie were always spotless. My Jewish mother paid special attention to this and took extra good care of her baby boy's every need. This was all that made my wonderful life so wonderful.

There were nights when I would hear my parents talking about their newly-found hardships in their new surroundings. They felt ill at ease because they were the only Jewish people in the neighborhood. The South African people spoke a language which they did not understand, and my parents spoke a language which the South African people did not understand. This caused much confusion and unhappiness. Particularly for Mama. During the violent persecution of the Jewish people in Russia by the Cossacks at the turn of the century, they had been residents in the city of Radvilisik in the state of Lithuania and beheld many atrocities there. My father had heard about a shipload of horses that was being exported to South Africa, and was able to arrange for both his family and his wife's family to work aboard the ship. Both families were Orthodox Jewish folk, my grandfather being a Jewish Rabbi.

My father found employment in the city of Johannesburg as a bartender. The wages were low but Mama continually thanked God for the bread on the table, and life that He had given to us all.

We were very well received into the Jewish school (synagogue) and it was my delight to run with the chickens in my hand every Friday night to the yard behind the synagogue where our Rabbi would say a blessing over the chickens and then slaughter them. It was a great thrill for the kids to watch these chickens kicking and flying around without their heads. The meat was now kosher.

I always looked forward to taking the Friday night meal to the Rabbi first. My sister was jealous so Mama used to allow her to light the candles instead. My elder brother was given the honor of saying the blessings over the food and sipping a little wine afterwards, so the three children were kept happy by happy parents.

Occasionally there would be an upset in the home when one of the family would report that one of the neighbors called them some filthy anti-semitic name. But, apart from this, and one or two other minor incidents, I found life sublime. Then one day so very unexpectedly it happened. My whole world came tumbling down. In one split second my popularity ceased. My happiness, joy and excitement vanished and a new life was forced on me.

The thing that took my popularity away was the Bible. For the first time the Bible was introduced to our class. The principal of the school had walked into our class. He was very proud to be able to announce to the class that Bible study would be given each morning to the class in the future. Little did I realize how that Bible study class would alter my life of victory to one of total defeat. But I went home to give Mama the news about the announcement that the school principal had made. Mama was thrilled and assured me that the word of God was what every Jewish boy should know. She also mentioned the Ten Commandments and other famous characters that she had learned about in the Talmud (Hebrew Bible). I felt happier about the new subject that we were going to be taught. I was going to come home each day and share my knowledge of God's word with Mama.

I shall never ever forget that day. The teacher that I had loved so much entered the classroom. As usual, she smiled and greeted everybody with such peace and happiness that it made everyone feel peaceful and happy right away. She paged through the pretty white Bible that she held so very gently in her hand. I became impatient. I wanted to know what God had to say through that book. "I want all the Jewish children to stand and leave the room immediately," I heard her say. For the moment I could not believe my ears and just sat there as though a train had smashed into the front of my desk. I could not move. I was flabbergasted.

The love of my life arose to her feet. "That means you too Hymie," she said with her usual smile, pointing her brightly polished finger at me. I watched the other Jewish kids leaving the room, and I wanted to ask for some sort of explanation. After all Mama had said that I should learn about God and Moses and a lot of other people in the Bible. But the smile had disappeared from her face. "Get out, Hymie Rubenstein," she commanded.

How I managed to get up and get out I do not know. The other Jewish kids just stood there staring at me, and I just stood there staring at them. I wanted to cry. I wanted to hide in a hole. My pride had taken a violent blow. From the top of the ladder I had fallen below the bottom rung. I walked away from the others and stood below the open window of the class on the other side of the building. I heard the teacher mention a name that I had never heard before. She mentioned it often. The name was Jesus. I strained my ears as I heard her tell of the disgraceful way that the Jews had mistreated this man and dragged him to a place called Golgotha and brutally nailed this man to an old rugged cross. Mama hadn't told me anything about that man. I was afraid that the teacher did not have the Bible that Mama quoted from, and I wondered if she had God's Bible at all. The Bible study came to a close and the rejected ones were called back into the class.

The whole atmosphere had now completely changed. It was as though a dark cloud had settled over the room. I had not ever experienced this type of feeling before. I looked at the non-Jews that had remained in the class, but it was obvious that they were just ignoring both me and the other Jewish kids. I sat down in my desk next to my mate. He moved to the very edge of the desk and practically fell off the thing in order to keep well away from me. As the days went on and the Bible classes continued, the dark cloud became a lot darker.

We had our school vacation and I had hoped that the Bible classes would no longer continue in the higher grade. My hopes were short-lived. We were not only advised that the Bible classes would continue, but that every Friday morning the senior classes would gather in the school hall for singing. I told Mama about this and she agreed that I should do my best to learn to sing so that I could one day either become a good doctor, or a good Cantor in the Synagogue.

Mama got me looking exceptionally smart for the first Friday school singing. I also added a little extra hair-cream to my pitch-black crop of hair, and a little more white to the sneakers. About five hundred children stood in the hall. One of the teachers announced that the morning meeting would be opened in prayer. He prayed very nicely for every teacher and every child, politician, and policeman in the city, county and land. I noticed that he ended his prayer mentioning the name of Jesus. I became afraid as I wondered what might happen in a gathering where that name was mentioned? It didn't take long for me to quit wondering. The principal walked in very spritely, smiling and waving his long arms up and down and around and about. Then he walked towards a large blackboard that I had not noticed standing at the end of the platform. He quickly commanded four young boys to lift the board and place it in the center of the platform so that everyone could see. "This is the first song that we will learn and sing," he said pointing to the blackboard.

"Read it aloud with me," he said as he tapped each word. "What a friend we have in Jesus" everyone read out aloud. I should say practically everyone. I cannot account for the other Jewish children, but I was afraid to even let the name pass over my lips. "I almost forgot," I heard the song leader announce. "All you Jewish kids leave the hall immediately, please." I had had a feeling that something would happen when that name Jesus was involved. My feeling was confirmed—it happened.

This time it did not have such a blasting effect as the first time, but it sure did have an effect. Not only upon me but upon the non-Jewish singers that had first been told that the Jewish people had killed Jesus, and now that the best friend they could ever have was crucified on Calvary.

I was now more mature than I was in that Bible study class, and I was all ready to quit school and let those non-Jews upset others but not me. After the singing was dismissed I noticed a group of kids had gathered and were beating up one of the Jewish kids that had left the hall. Some of them noticed me and shouted aloud, "You dirty Christ killer, you killed Jesus!" It didn't take my feet long to realize that if I wanted to avoid being beaten up by those furious boys and girls, I had better run as fast as I possibly could. I managed to outrun the group, and got home panting hard and out of breath. I was thankful that they had not caught me. I was sure from their behavior that they intended doing some real damage to my body.

I walked into my bedroom completely and totally defeated. I sat down on my small bed unable to comprehend all these things that had taken place because of a Bible, and a man named Jesus. I heard my mother call my name as she entered my room. My mother only spoke Yiddish and asked me why I had not come into the kitchen to kiss her? This was my daily custom. I apologized and said that I had forgotten. "My baby doesn't forget his Mama," she laughed as she bent over and kissed me on my head. I felt so sure that if there was anyone who could help me at that very moment there was nobody better than my Mama.

"Mama," I said, "can I ask you a very special question?" She looked at me and asked me why I had been running. "You are out of breath, my son." She touched my heart. "Vat is it?" she asked in her best broken English, her hand still pressed against my heart.

"Mama, did I kill a man by the name of Jesus?" I

lovingly inquired.

My mother suddenly altered her stand, and with the hand that was once pressed lovingly against my heart, slapped me viciously in the mouth and began shaking my head wildly by the ears. *"Giam"* (My Jewish name for Life) she yelled at the top of her voice, I forbid you to ever mention that name in this house again." She then began spitting on the floor and wringing her hands frantically as though I had done some unpardonable thing. She continued commanding me to have nothing whatsoever to do with the Christian children. To associate only with the Yiddisha kids and to leave the *Goyim* (Gentiles) alone. According to Mama there were only two types of people: Jews or Christians.

"Who was this man Mama?" I asked, afraid to mention the name. Mama walked towards the door and began yelling at the top of her voice again. "A good-for-nothing loafer. A liar and a thief," she shouted. Mama was really annoyed.

I immediately came to one conclusion that apart from not knowing who this Jesus was, whoever He was, He most certainly was getting me into a lot of trouble. I often thought that it would be wise to change my name to some name that was not so obviously Jewish.

I attended *Gaida* (Hebrew school) regularly, and many an afternoon after the class we would inquire about and discuss the Christian people. We heard many strange and weird stories about the Imposter who called himself Jesus, the Son of God. Not knowing any different we believed that He walked the streets of Jerusalem with His twelve buddies, and used to enter the synagogues during the services, beat up all the members there, and then steal the money out of the treasury. We used to laugh and clap hands as each one in turn would tell a story. One would then compose a dirty recitation about the Imposter, and all would laugh again. One story that used to get good applause was the one where Jesus and His men used to go to the Sea of Galilee on a Friday night and roll large boulders into the water. On the Saturday morning they used to collect a large crowd of people together and then Jesus would jump from one stone to the other to give the people the impression that He was walking on water.

During one of the high holy holidays (*Yom Kippur*)

Day of Atonement, our Rabbi made a very special announcement. He said financially the synagogue was in very poor shape. The rent was very difficult to come by, and that he personally was not receiving the income that he deserved. Then he said that if things would not better themselves, and the members would not give financial support, the building would have to be vacated. "How would you like to see the *Magon David* (Star of David) that is fixed to the front of the building removed, and the Christian cross there in its place?" he shouted. By the time the service was ended a special collection was called for and the building fully paid.

I became a good young member of the Jewish synagogue, and both my brother and I were given special privileges to open and close the Ark during services. I loved to sing along with the others as the procession walked down the center of the synagogue, allowing the members that so desired to come forward and kiss the scroll or scrolls. The ceremony used to let me feel so close to God. I never failed to take my *Talis* (Shawl) and touch the plate that hung from the Scroll. The plate was inscribed with the Laws of Moses. Then I would kiss the place where the shawl had touched the plate. It thrilled me every time I did it.

After much reading of the Scriptures from the scroll the Rabbi would then return to the Ark to replace the Holy Scrolls. Once again the members that so desired would go forward and pay respects to God by kissing His word. When the scrolls were replaced in the Ark, I would pull my gold cord with the heavy tassels and the Ark would be sheltered under a beautiful and heavily designed gold and silver curtain. My brother and I would then walk to the chairman, who in turn would offer us a pinch of snuff, and thank us for our help. We always took pleasure in doing what we could to help in the synagogue, and apart from paying our tithe, we were taught by our father to always give liberally. "God gives to those that give to Him, my sons," he would say.

Dad was far to busy earning a living for his family. He received certain stock market tips from some of his customers, and he thoroughly enjoyed dealing in gold shares. Through this he bought his own hotel.

The Milner Park Hotel was on the small side with twelve

bedrooms, but an exceptionally large dining room and kitchen. We were so happy that we now had a hotel of our very own, and also thought that we would now be able to see more of Papa. But our ideas never materialized. My father was practically day and night in the bar. At the beginning he was unable to afford to hire assistance. Later he was unable to carry on without rest so Mama had to take a turn in the bar. She detested alcohol, but my father tried to convince her that it was necessary for the hotel proprietor to drink with the customers, "For the good of the business," he would say. Many nights Dad would come upstairs very inebriated and we could hear him and mother arguing terribly.

Mama's side of the business was exceptionally good. The meals were always perfect, and the Kosher dishes that she made occasionally just thrilled the residents, and the visitors. It also started attracting more business.

It would thrill us to sit in the bar and watch Papa put an extra shine on the bottles and the glasses. Sometimes he would give me a bottle and a cloth and say, "Shine it my baby, everything that can shine must shine."

Mama was very *Froom* (Orthodox). No cutlery or crockery that was used for meat dishes could be used for fish or milk dishes. Everything had to be blessed by the Rabbi and stamped "Kosher" before we were permitted to eat it. One day Mama took ill with a very bad cold. The doctor called and prescribed some tablets, but she grew worse. The doctor kept coming more frequently and doing all that he knew how to help Mama regain her strength. But with all his help and suggestions she contracted pneumonia, which in a short time turned to double pneumonia and Mama died. For three hundred and sixty-five days after her death my brother and I never failed once to go to the synagogue to say *"Kiddish"* (prayer for the dead). We missed our mother for she took such excellent care of us all.

Chapter Two

Soldier of the King

The year was 1939, and the eyes of the world were upon Germany and her leader, Adolph Hitler. Britain had declared war against Germany. King George of Britain had appealed to South Africa to do likewise as it was a member of the British commonwealth.

Many anti-German demonstrations took place in Johannesburg, and I was one of the front-line offenders. At the age of nineteen my soul was crying for adventure and excitement, and here was the opportunity to allow it all to blow out. My older friends were now joining the forces, and the song, "We are soldiers of the King" was on every lip.

When I saw how smart my friends looked in their bright Scottish uniforms, and how proud they were of the rifles they carried, I felt that somehow I just had to join them. But when I saw the fuss the girls made over them I went to the recruiting office and asked for an application form to join the First Transvaal Scottish Regiment. I took the application to my dad. With tears streaming down his eyes he told me that he expected something like that from me. He gathered me in his arms and said, "My boy, take good care of yourself, and God be with you." He signed the papers and left the room weeping.

After a few weeks of training we had a farewell parade through the city. I felt as though everyone had gathered there to see me. In time to the bagpipes we marched through the streets, and I got an extra swing on my kilts while the girls threw flowers and confetti at us. All the "good-bye kisses" eventually came to an end, and as I collected my "battle-kit" from the Quarter Master Store, I realized that the fun and frolic times were now over. There was a war to fight and a war to win.

As our troop train moved slowly out of the station for

"destination unknown," it slowly dawned on me that all the glamour, bright lights, pretty girls, dancing and gaiety times had now come to an end. Members of my family stood there with thousands of others waving handkerchiefs and weeping. I felt like weeping myself. Instead I walked back into my compartment and asked if any of my fellow soldiers had a beer. Somebody pushed a bottle of brandy into my hand saying, "Drink a man's drink, man." Seven pairs of eyes watched me anxiously to see what my reaction would be. Without any hesitation I decided to join my future life-long buddies as a hardened drinker.

I might have been on the young side, but one thing I was never afraid to put my fists behind my mouth. So when I now began to drink as much as the others (if not more) they made sure that they did not upset me in any way.

One day the train came to a halt and the company commanders ordered everyone to de-train. We had arrived at our destination at a place called Cullinan. (The Cullinan diamond, the largest diamond in the world was found here.) This was where we were going to set up our camp. It was nothing but trees and long green grass for miles and miles. If ever there was a heartbreaking sight to behold, that was it. Truck loads of shovels and picks arrived from somewhere, and when the command came for everyone to grab a pick and shovel I made a quick turnabout and walked into the thick bush giving the impression that I was unbuckling my belt. The whole afternoon I could hear picks and shovels pounding into the hard earth. At sunset it was quiet, apart from sergeants and corporals shouting out one order after the other.

The morning bugler awoke me from a sound sleep. I knew that I would have to forsake my hiding place as I could hear the "roll call" being given. I walked into my section and all the guys wanted to know where I had been. I noticed that a lot of tents had been erected and I complimented them on their fine work.

"Rubenstein, are you here?" I heard the company sergeant screaming. "Yes, sergeant, here I am," I screamed back. "Why don't you answer your ---- name when I call your ---- name?" he yelled back. I remained silent as he called the names of Rabinsky, Rappaport, Shapiro, Steinberg,

16

Tannenbaum and Van Der Westhuizen. I gathered that I was not the only Yiddisha Scotchman in the company.

"In one hours time you will be on parade, fully shaven, fully cleaned, and fully fed," the sergeant commanded quickly. I was still trying to digest what he had said when he hollered, "And that goes for you too, Private Rubenstein." I wondered why he picked on me?

We now began to get down to more of a war-like way. We got instruction in bayonet charging, Vickers guns, mortar guns, and hand-grenade throwing. One afternoon we were informed that we would be moving further north for further training. This time we were packed into three and five-ton trucks like cattle. The seats were hard and the roads were rough and dusty. At the most unexpected times somebody would produce a bottle of either brandy or whiskey from their kit bags, and that did have the tendency to overcome much of the discomfort.

It took the convoy two days to arrive at it's destination. Barberton was a place situated in very mountainous country, and when we realized that we had to start all over again to build yet another army camp it was far from encouraging. But discouraged or encouraged, we had to build once again. This time it was not a camp with many tents, but we had to build long, large bungalows to accomodate sixty soldiers. It kept the men very busy and the work was very hard.

Personally, I did not care for hard work so I just had to find a way out. Like an answer to prayer a notice was placed on the bulletin board instructing everyone who was interested in boxing to report to Sgt. Gerry Walker. I threw down my bag of nails, and the hammer that had been issued to me and ran to find the sergeant. He didn't greet me very cordially, and accused me of "swinging the lead" (dodging hard work). I told him about my boxing days in school and how I loved the sport. It did not have the effect I hoped that it would. He continued to eye me very suspiciously. "Colonel Kirby is very keen that we produce a Scottish team of boxers that will beat any other battalion in the regiment," he informed me. He then instructed me to report to Sergeant Major Mack of "A" company.

I reported to Sgt. Major Mack. His breath smelled as

though he had already celebrated a victory, and he was quite impressed with my first workout. We met in the Officer's Mess later that night to discuss different strategies in the boxing business with some of the interested officers. I felt real good to be amongst the "higher brass." I had quite a few brandies with Mack and promised him that I would quit drinking immediately and go into hard training for the competition that had been scheduled against the Armoured Car Division.

The night arrived for our match against the Armoured Car Division. There was much excitement. This was the first time a boxing tournament had been arranged. Mack was my manager, and he assured me that he knew my opponent personally and that he was no match for me. I knew he was lying, but I appreciated his encouraging words.

Sergeant Robinson was introduced first as the light-heavyweight champion of the Armoured Car Division. When I heard that he was a sergeant, I made up my mind to whip him, and whip him real good. We met in the center of the ring as the bell sounded. Mack had instructed me to go like ----from the sound of the bell. That strategy seemed to startle Robinson who wanted to dance and feel out his opponent. We got into a clinch and he held on to me tightly. I complained to the referee, but he told me to "Shut up and keep fighting." This added to my temper, and I attacked the sergeant with both fists flying like crazy through the air. One of the blows struck him and he fell to his knees. Every Scottish and Jewish soldier jumped to his feet screaming, "Kill him, Hymie, kill him, Hymie."

The bell sounded and the first round was over. I returned to my corner and Mack told me to do what everyone else had told me to do: "Kill him, Hymie." He removed my gum-guard and gave me a drink of cool water, then threw another sponge of water into my face and yet another down my hot sweating back.

I felt as fresh as I did when I started. The bell sounded for the second round, and the last thing that Mack said was, "Kill him dead now." My supporters were screaming for a "Knock the --- out of the ring, Hymie." I decided to do just that, but my opponent hindered me by holding on for dear

18

life. "Let my arms go you ----," I screamed at him, but it seemed as though he didn't hear me. Much to my surprise Sergeant Robinson fell to his knees, fell flat on his face and then rolled over onto his back. I knew that I hadn't hit him, but the crowd went mad, and many of my buddies jumped into the ring kissing and hugging me for that "Knock-out punch I landed . . ."

The Colonel sent his personal congratulations to me, and I thought that I might become a major over night. Instead I was sent with the rest of the boxers to a place on the border called Komatipoort to rest for a while, and then get into hard training again for the tournament against the Irish Regiment.

The boxing team returned to Barberton for the final weigh-in. I fasted that day to make sure that I scaled in at the right weight. I scaled in right on the dot, 175 pounds. Any weight above 175 would have classified me a heavy-weight.

The camps, Irish and Scottish, were seething with great excitement. There was very little love lost between the two regiments and the one was always trying to outsmart the other. At one time the Irish regiment went on a route march for three days. A week later the Scottish regiment went on one for four days. The results of the boxing tournament would have a big bearing on future conditions.

I had a big meal in the afternoon and waited for the evening to arrive. By the time that I had been introduced to the armies as the light-heavyweight boxing champion of the Scottish Regiment   pandemonium had broken out. There had been many fights amongst the spectators. One referee had been badly assaulted for what some Scotchmen had thought to be the wrong decision. I felt a little nervous, but my manager, Mack was right there to say the right words of encouragement, as usual. "I know that ---- personally, Hymie, and he is no match for you. You just get in there like the last time and kill the -----."

I looked across the other corner of the ring and spotted my opposition. He was a tall blonde lad, strongly built, and he had many advisers and massagers all around him. He seemed to be cool. I promised myself to see to it that I got a little bit of heat under him quickly. The gong sounded and the last thing I heard Mack yell was, "Fly at him Hymie and kill the -----." I wanted to repeat my surprise attack that upset Sergeant Robinson a few weeks before, but blonde Corporal Muller danced away from me. I stalked him but he kept dancing away and smiling at me at the same time. We traded punches in the middle of the ring and his punches seemed to be packed with power. I decided to dance around a bit myself to make sure that I kept my confidence. The wild screaming and shouting from the soldiers made me feel real good.

Most unexpectedly something hammered me on the side of my head. I didn't see it come but I felt right where it landed. It rocked me. The crowd went wild. For the moment I thought that somebody had thrown a rock at me from the audience, and when Muller closed in I grabbed him by the arms. As he pushed me away, another rock hit me right in the right eye, and staggered me badly. I felt that he had hit all the life out of me. The sound of the bell was the loveliest sound that I had ever heard. I got back to my corner hurting real bad. Mack took out my gum-guard and frantically started washing me down and giving me instructions. "Please throw in the towel Mack," I begged. "This guy will kill me." Mack just patted me on the back and said, "Come on, Hymie, now you have got that --- stone cold." When my manager assured me that I had my opposition stone cold I took new courage and decided to put an end to the fight right there and then.

The bell went for the second round. Muller did everything but kill me. He closed the only other eye that I had to see out of. He crashed his fist into my nose and caused blood to come streaming out, and as the bell sounded he hit me full in the mouth, causing my lips to blow up like a balloon. Mack rushed over to the corner that I was in to take me to the right corner. I slumped into the chair. I was sure that Mack was well aware of my condition, and that he would throw in the towel. But he began washing me and giving me further instructions. "Please, Mack," I pleaded, "Throw that --- towel in." Mack once more patted me on the back. "Have you gone mad?" he shouted at me. "That fellow will not last another round with you." Mack was my manager and friend.

I respected him and his knowledge of the boxing game. If Mack said that I had Muller, "stone cold" then I had Muller stone cold. The bell rang for the third and final round. I jumped up quickly with the help of Mack and in the far distance I spotted a tall young blonde giant coming towards me. I knew that I had plans right there and then to see the fight through, but those plans failed as a bigger rock than before hit me on the side of my jaw.

I woke up the following morning in the hospital. Apparently Corporal Muller had hit me with such force that my legs flew up in the air. I landed on my head and was removed from the ring unconscious. It was worth it. The hospital bed was so white and clean and so comfortable. I was working out a plan to keep my unconsciousness for the rest of the war. A beautiful blonde nurse came to talk with me. I didn't like blondes since the Muller incident, but this was a female one and I loved her right away. I had practically forgotten what beauty and cleanliness looked like. With a big, shiney, bright, white-teeth smile she asked, "How are you feeling, Joe Louis?" I appreciated the humour but I couldn't smile, neither could I answer the question. My entire face was puffed up and very painful. "The doctor wants you to go for X-Rays first thing tomorrow," she said as she busied herself adjusting the bandages that somebody had placed under my chin and over my head. "You might have a fractured jaw, sonny boy," she continued as she rubbed some salve around both my eyes. "Take a good look at yourself," she laughed as she held up a mirror in front of me. The other patients all laughed aloud. I got a fright as I failed to recognize myself. I wondered if that was the way a man looked after he had fallen out of a plane about twenty to thirty thousand feet high? She laid my sore head back on the big white pillow and covered me with the big white sheet.

When I thought of ever returning to that camp again and sleeping on that hard floor called "mother earth," under thick hard military blankets again, I hoped that I not only had a fractured jaw, but that it and my other injuries would never heal. After the x-rays the doctor said that I was lucky that my jaw was all right. I disagreed mentally. Somehow I had to figure out a way that I could remain in that hospital.

Preferably for the duration of the war.

The following day the doctor came through the ward inspecting all the patients. When I heard him instruct the nurse, "Discharge this man tomorrow," I became afraid that I might have the same sentence passed upon me, but I was so very happy when he told the nurse that I would have to stay a few days longer.

Blondie arrived with the afternoon shift and washed me because they had failed to wash me that morning owing to the x-rays that I had to have. It was the first time since my Yiddisha Mama washed me in the kitchen sink, that a lady had touched my body with soap and water. Blondie knew that I loved it, and quickly pulled her hand away as my fingers closed around her small dainty hand. I thought that she might rebuke me, but she didn't. She gently tucked me in, gave me a few pills and water and stroked me on the forehead very softly. "See you later, Tarzan," I heard her say as I fell into a deep sleep.

The food was excellent, and after five days the doctor suggested that I might return to my unit. I complained that I got terribly dizzy when I walked. This seemed to bother him. It didn't bother me because it wasn't true.

Blondie and I began meeting every second day at eleven o'clock sharp. We met at the laundry room where "out of bed patients" and nurses did the washing. I was sure that we fell in love. But it didn't seem to be the same love that I had for my girl back home. She told me that she was from New Zealand and thought that I was the nicest patient that she had ever dated. I told her that she was the nicest nurse that I ever dated. She suggested that I accompany her to the officer's dance the coming Saturday night. I told her that she knew full well that I was no officer, and that the penalty for un-officially wearing an officer's uniform was severe. "Anything from life in jail to being thrown out of the army," I told her. "Come on Tarzan, you're not afraid are you?" she teased. "What is more, Hymie, I have a major's uniform that will just fit you!" I was dumbfound for a moment. "Tomorrow I will bring it here and you can go into the engine room and try it on. I have to go now, Major Rubenstein!" We kissed and she hurried off to her daily duties.

I didn't sleep that night. If ever my head was causing trouble it was now. I didn't want to show heartbreak that I was frightened out of my wits, and wondered if it would not be wise for me to tell the doctor at the following inspection that I felt fine, and would like to return to my unit? The following morning the doctor arranged for me to visit a Colonel that would examine me for my head pains.

That morning everyone seemed to be overflowing with excitement. I noticed that even those that had been certified as "unfit for duty" cases, were walking about, and others rushing in and out of the ward that at one time could not walk about without the help of crutches. "What's happening?" I screamed as I jumped out of bed to join in all the excitement. "The Fifth Brigade is moving out to the front lines, and every able-bodied soldier is needed." Patients were just jumping into whatever vehicle they could to get back to their units. Others rushed to the Quarter Master Stores to retrieve their belongings, and all red tape and organization vanished. Nobody was waiting to fill in any forms of "Release," or, "Fit for duty." The move everyone was so impatiently waiting for had come. "Front line action." I grew just as excited as everyone else.

I had also been looking forward to the time that the play, play war would be over, and that the real thing would come along. Well, here it was. I knew that my little love affair was over at the same time, but I knew that my little New Zealand blonde nurse, would understand. I inquired about her from office to office, but there was such a panic going on with the hospital staff, that nobody paid any attention to me. I began panicking even more when I thought that there might be the chance that I could not say "Goodbye, honey" and depart with a big kiss to remember her by. I ran up to the Colonel's office where I was supposed to have my head checked and thought that I might find her there. Neither the Colonel nor the nurse was there. I ran down to the laundry hoping that she might be there waiting for me. She wasn't there either. I ran to the nurses mess hoping that she would be there enjoying breakfast. She wasn't there. I ran from tent to tent, from ward to ward, from bungalow to

23

bungalow. I found some nurses still in bed, others half dressed, others not dressed, and the shouts and curses some greeted me with did not in any way help to cool off the panic that had gripped me. The whole hospital was practically deserted. I thrilled as I spotted a short blonde nurse running towards a truck filled with soldiers. I rushed over to grab her. My heart sank. It wasn't my girl. "This is the last bus to the Fifth Brigade Camp" I heard the driver shout.

I was transfered to the Transport Company from the Vickers Support Company as there was a shortage of truck drivers. I was thrilled about this as I always did want to have a car of my own. Now I had my own three-ton truck. Most of the trucks were used to carry personnel. My truck was used to carry food supplies. My luck. Every driver wanted to drive the food-supplies truck. The reason was obvious. "You're just a lucky Jew," my buddies would tell me. I told them that God was good to the Jews and to the food-supply drivers. There was much moaning about the discomfort in those three and five-ton steel trucks. But I enjoyed my comfort in a soft-padded cab. For days we travelled North, and although our destination was unknown, we knew that the Italian Army was in Ethiopia. The Italians had joined the German forces.

After a few days we arrived at the Capital of Kenya, Nairobe. We rested for a few days and had our food, gasoline, ammunition and guns replenished. I fell in love with a six-foot tall thermometer that had been fixed to a wall alongside a large pharmacy. That thing just fascinated me as I had never seen one that size. I took it as a souvenir the day the convoy moved out and fixed it to the back of my cab. When others saw the thermometer on my truck they all said how they had wanted to remove it. One officer wanted to buy the thing from me, but I told him that it was given to me as a keepsake, and that I was taught by my little Jewish mother to never ever give away keepsakes. This made him mad, but the officers and the higher ranks now became a lot friendlier towards the rank and file who now had more guns and ammunition and hand-grenades than what they could handle.

One day the order came through that the supply trucks

were to fall back and join the troops a day later. It was now apparent that we were going into action.

We handed every soldier extra packets of cigarettes and emergency rations. I sat comfortably in my cab waving my buddies on to war. By the look that some of them gave me I felt that they just didn't care much for my send-off. I couldn't worry about them. I had my own job to do, and it was just as important as theirs. I had to keep that truck running and clean. "Where would they be without me and my truck and the goods?" I told myself.

A day later when we moved up into jungle country I really felt sorry for the boys in those trucks. There were truck tracks everywhere. Trees, hedges, branches and vines lay everywhere. The terrain was scattered with large boulders and rocks. I wondered how many of the trucks would last under those conditions? Late that night we drove into a forest. The name of the place was Marzabit Forest. It was as black as ink in there, and we were ordered to paint our headlamp glasses with only a four-inch by two-inch opening for light, it made driving a nightmare. There were military police trying to direct somebody somewhere, but it was apparent that they themselves knew very little of who was where and what was what. The Quarter Master who was riding with me told me to "Pull off anywhere." I pulled off anywhere very nearly riding over men that had bedded down for the night. I noticed a large tree to my right and pulled up right against it. "I'll go and find Lieutenant Bailey. You stay right here Rubenstein," he commanded. I didn't want to tell him how ridiculous his idea was in case he changed his mind.

I longed for a can of cling peaches, and a mug full of strong "Army Ration Rum." Once he had left it didn't take me long to open the canvas on the side where I knew full well I could lay my hands easily on what I desired. I sat in my comfortable cab thinking about the possibility that there were angels taking extra good care of me. As I predicted, the Quarter Master quit his ridiculous search only five minutes after leaving the truck. He spent the night in another truck as he couldn't find his way back to mine.

Early the next morning before "reveille" had sounded

I was rudely awakened by Lieutenant Bailey with curses and shouts because my truck was about twelve miles from where he wanted it to be. Under his directions, I moved the truck to the position that he chose. The Quarter Master found me a few hours later and cursed me for moving the truck without his permission. The Regimental Sergeant Major eventually arrived and blamed me for the soldiers not having their quinine rations which were on the truck and which was the "First Command" given by Command Headquarters on arrival in the Forest. "If the men die of malaria you will be court martialed for it, you stupid, ignorant dummy," he yelled at me. My buddies laughed and asked why I didn't knock him out like the Irishman knocked me out? I didn't appreciate their wisecracks, but I got busy handing out the quinine pills.

It was a busy day for me. I also had to hand out small one-man tents with mosquito nets and gloves to each man. Then the cook got hold of me to get dry wood and build him a large fire to cook on. The forest was wet and damp and mosquito infested. To find dry wood was like finding a needle in a haystack. But I knew what would happen if I didn't find what "Cookie" looked for.

I remembered that the thermometer that I had taken as a souvenir was mounted on some real thick lumber. All I needed to do was to please "Cookie." Those angels must have been there with me. I found an old boat half submerged and half out of a dirty mud pool of water. How that ever got there only God knew. I could never in my wildest dreams imagine anyone boating in that part of the whole wide world. But I pulled out my bayonet and hacked a whole pile of dry wood for "Cookie." He didn't appreciate me taking so long to bring him dry wood. I knew that it was fruitless to try and tell him what he didn't know about finding dry wood in a wet forest.

The men were thrilled to receive a good hot meal, and there was no ration on the "Army Issue Rum." Those who remembered to take their quinine and get under their tents and wear their gloves and put on their mosquito nets that night were very few. "Army Issue" kept them warm, and by the strength that it had I was sure that if a mosquito bit me

26

it would die.

Up until this point the enemy had not yet been contacted, but the "Advance Guard" had been away four days. Early one morning the order came through, "Prepare to move." Every man was first given an extra food ration and an extra pouch of hand-grenades. The supply truck had to wait twelve hours before moving off. As we moved off the next day men from the signal corps advised us that the Italian forces had been contacted and that there was heavy fighting on the front. "Let us get up there and feed our men," I suggested to my travelling companion. The Quarter Master told me that he intended to "Stick strictly to orders."

I knew that he was afraid to get too near to the action, and as I heard the rat-a-tat of the Vicker's guns, the explosion of the mortars, and the shelling of the Howitzers I longed to be with my buddies on the machine guns. Mega Fort was an Italian stronghold in Ethiopia. After hours of constant attack the enemy surrendered. The days that followed were busy ones for everybody. Prisoners had to be recorded and fed. Enemy supplies had to either be destroyed or listed. The souvenir hunters were busy too. I had now been promoted to sergeant and this helped me to have more time to wander about souvenir hunting. "Cookie" was too busy cooking to enjoy looking about the captured area, so I promised him the first Lugar gun I found. I found many souvenirs, but no guns. A friend of mine who was boasting with the gun he had found shot off his middle finger accidentally. There was talk of sending him back to South Africa because of the incident. When I heard that a man could get home if his finger was shot off, I began to get ideas. These ideas stopped very soon. The fellow that lost his finger lost his life too. Gangrene had set in. There were three other cases of self-inflicted wounds. They died the same way. There were very few casualties in the battle of Mega Fort, thanks to the quick surrender by the enemy.

The signal corps had informed us that our other division had captured Addis Ababa, the capital of Ethiopia, whose leader was Heili Salasi. So there was great rejoicing in the ranks for the victories on every side, with Sergeant Rubenstein playing an important part in the celebration.

I had been given complete charge of "rum ration." This helped me obtain souvenirs without searching for them. For an extra issue of rum or an extra packet of cigarettes, some of the men would give away their very lives. My truck was loaded with what they craved for, and I added some fine trophies to both "Cookie's" collection and mine.

When the cook was your friend, you had the best friend in the army. I ate well, drank well and lived well. I appreciated it even more when I saw how some of the fellows looked after a day out reconnoitering for miles around.

Every night was a drunken party for those who wanted a drunken party. There were very few who didn't want them. I indulged every night without fail. I became quite an entertainer.

It was rumored that the Division would soon be moving up into Egypt to remove the Germans from occupying the whole of North Africa. The rumor soon materialized, but the moving of the Germans took a long time, longer than we had anticipated, and many valuable lives were lost in the effort.

Our base camp was called Helwan. It was about thirty miles to the south of Cairo. I discovered there was a train that ran into Cairo, and like the rest, I wanted to see the city we had heard so much about.

When I heard there was a New Zealand Hospital on the banks of the Nile River that flowed through Cairo, I immediately reported sick—complained of serious backache. I had been informed that doctors found it very difficult to diagnose this type of complaint.

Day after day I reported sick. Everyone was given a number "nine" regardless. This pill had a drastic effect on the bowels. Many of the sick quit reporting "sick" because of this. But I persevered and eventually was sent to the hospital in Cairo.

I hoped that I would find the girl I left behind in the hospital in Nairobe, Kenya. But the authorities had not even known of the hospital there.

I went through different treatments and disposed of different pills, and went dancing in the Cabarets at night. Cairo was so very mystical and strange. I loved sneaking out of the hospital each night, and going into that dark "air raid"- proof city. I got into the massage department of the hospital and that helped me keep fit for the dancing at night.

Suddenly it all came to a stop.

General Rommel had broken through the British lines in the desert, untold numbers of wounded were being evacuated to Cairo and the hospitals there. I was immediately discharged as "fit for service," and instructed to make my way back to the base camp.

I noticed an ambulance standing outside the hospital gate and the driver informed me that he was going to the base camp with many other patients from the hospital. I noticed that there were many still heavily bandaged, and others on crutches that were being vacated. I quickly rushed back into the hospital to get myself a pair of crutches as a souvenir.

The camp was full of talk about going into the front lines soon. I knew full well that the name of Hymie Rubenstein was amongst that group, but I was in no hurry to see more action in the Western Desert.

I hobbled out of the ambulance with the others, and they were all herded into a hall where the Sergeant Major said how sorry he was to see them. "Derelicts shouldn't be sent up to the front," he screamed. The names and numbers were taken of the derelicts and they were excused any duties. They were also excused "roll call" in the mornings. No reporting and no roll call excited my little Jewish heart.

I wanted to visit Israel so badly and mentioned it to another young Jewish man who was an Air Force mechanic, he had been discharged from the hospital and could not find his squadron. He readily agreed to take full advantage of his "lost" condition.

We both hobbled down to the main road, buried our crutches and caught a taxi to the Helwan Station. From Cairo we started hitchhiking with different convoys all along the Suez Canal, and finally caught an overloaded train to the Holy Land.

I spent two months going from city to city, drinking from bar to bar. My Air Force friend had left me because he did not approve of my vicious drinking and fighting.

He made the final decision in a Cabaret where a very attractive young Jewish girl was singing "blue songs." In a drunken state I jumped up on the platform and commanded her to sing, "Begin the Begin." Unfortunately the young lady could not understand what I was trying to tell her, and the leader of the band told me she did not know the tune.

In a rage I turned about and kicked a hole through the drum. The saxophonist hit me across the eye with his instrument, and this was like a bomb setting off a "free for all."

As the Military Police entered I vacated the premises via the nearest window.

When I found that my money-book had run dry, I decided to return to Cairo and then to base. My regiment had moved up into the Alexandria area. For two days I hitchhiked from Cairo to Alexandria where I found my regiment. The tents had been dug into the ground about ten feet deep to prevent anyone getting hurt by bomb shrapnel. I was glad that I missed all that work. Or, I thought that I had missed it. The Sergeant Major upon being told that I had arrived back in the regiment, paid me a visit and placed me under "close arrest" for desertion. My punishment was to dig in officer's tents. It was hard work.

I was kept in the "prison tent" every night with seven big Nigerian soldiers. Some nights the fellows would smuggle in a bottle and that would help pass the evenings.

One day I was informed that my brother Len had come to visit me. His regiment (the Imperial Light Horse Brigade) had arrived in Egypt in support of the Allied forces. He was sorry to find me in jail, but we sure were glad to meet again. Len went into action. He was captured and went into "Prisoner of War Camp 54" in Rieti, Italy. He stayed there for twelve months and was transferred to Stalag 18A in Graz, Austria, for another twenty-four months.

Soon our battalion was alerted to leave for the front lines. A new dimension had taken place. The fun and joking and laughter had disappeared. It got even more serious as many ambulances and wounded passed us on their way back to base. A few days later we arrived at Mersa Matruh where we camouflaged our trucks and once again started to "dig in." This time the holes had to be made "as deep as possible." Night after night the German Air Force bombed us. This new experience was most unpleasant.

The air-raids increased.

I had contracted a big, red, nasty boil on the inside of my leg. It caused all the glands in my body to swell and I was paralyzed. To get to the doctor was practically an impossibility from where we were dug in, and there were so many wounded being brought in daily that I was sure I would just lie there in the sand and die.

One night I took my .303 rifle and tried to hold it in a position that I could shoot it right through that boil on my leg. My buddies did the best they could to help me by pouring gallons of brandy down my throat. Even that failed to help after a while.

One of the Scottish soldiers came to pay me a visit from another company. Max Wilson told me he specialized in removing boils. He took a look at mine and laughed. "This baby will come out like a baby," he said.

"How?" I questioned.

"Just you give me permission to take it out and 100 packets of cigarettes and the job is as good as done," he laughed.

I would have given him 100 times 100 cigarettes to get that thing out.

I accepted the terms. The boys all stood around to watch my reactions. Max Wilson first took his cigarettes then told me to get as much alcohol in as possible and that he would be back in one hours time. I wondered if he would return, but he did.

This time he was carrying a large empty bottle. He showed me the bottle and said, "This is the finest extractor the world has ever known." Everyone just stared at him as I lay there hopeless in the sand waiting to be "operated" on. One of the other men had brought a boiling pot of water from the kitchen nearby. Max Wilson placed a large towel into the boiling water. I became scared and told that he could have the cigarettes. From fright I was sobering up. "Please, leave me alone," I screamed.

31

Suddenly six or seven of the soldiers standing around fell on top of me and the last thing I felt before fainting was a red hot thing being plunged into that nasty over-ripe boil. Mr. Wilson had taken the cold bottle and placed the neck against my leg. Then he had wrapped the boiling hot towel around the cold bottle which in turn caused a vacuum that sucked the boil right out of my leg.

How long I lay unconscious I do not know, but it took me another full week to be able to walk. I am sure I would have died if Max Wilson hadn't come to my rescue. Or, maybe that angel I always joked about was there. The doctor had eventually managed to pay our section a visit. He was shocked to find me in such a weak state, and arranged to have me evacuated back to the base in Alexandria.

There were too many dead and dying for me to stay long in the hospital so I returned to the base camp for light duties.

I was given a light gasoline truck to drive. It was far from those happy days I had driving the food truck. Every day at one o'clock sharp Gerrie (German) Stuka planes would come and bomb our gasoline supplies. We could time their coming by the clock. Our own Air Force at that time seemed to be unable to hold off the German raiders.

We decided to set a trap for Gerrie one afternoon. One of the drivers hid in the kitchen with a Bren Gun. He would shoot the plane down as it pulled out of its usual dive. One o'clock arrived, and so did Gerrie, but this time instead of bombing the supply line he began to throw hand-grenades at us from the cockpit of the plane. As he pulled out of his dive just above the kitchen, driver McGregor opened up with his Bren Gun. Unbeknown to us there was a machine-gunner in the tail end of the plane, and he practically blew the whole of our kitchen away. We found McGregor lying there more shocked than anything else.

Suddenly one day there was an extraordinary roar in the sky. Row after row of Allied planes flew overhead. Some with the Royal Air Force insignia and others with the United States of America signia. This had a wonderful effect on each soldier.

General Rommel was having difficulty in getting gas

supplies as far down as he had come with German armor. This proved to be the turning point in the battle for the Western Desert.

I had not fully recovered and was sent up the line to Mersa Matruh. I was attached to the Royal Navy and it was my duty to see that their supplies were never short. It was like old times again driving the supply truck, but supplies here were not as plentiful. At times there were no supplies at all. I found myself an Italian delivery three-wheel tricycle that the Italians had left behind. I used it for small deliveries, until one day in a drunken stupor I stepped on the accelerator instead of the brake and flew off the dock right into the sea with it.

One day the adjutant of the unit detailed me to go to Benghazi railway station to collect the new company Colonel that had flown up from home base. I found that the reason that I had been chosen, much to the disgust of other senior ranks in the company, was because the new Colonel was Jewish. They had detailed the Jew to go and welcome the Jew.

This was a full day's travel, and it took much hard work to get my small truck in good shape and clean. So once I made ready and bid farewell to the rest of the men I set out for Benghazi. The road ran close to the Mediterranean Ocean. It was hot, muggy and very bumpy and dusty. Nevertheless, I was glad to get away from the camp. That evening just about sunset I arrived at my destination. It reminded me of bees round a honey pot.

Everybody seemed to be converging on a tent that stood somewhere in the middle of everything. There were trucks, tents, and all types of armoured vehicles standing in all directions, and soldiers, sailors and Air Force men everywhere. I dusted off my three stripes to show my authority in this mad war. I walked smartly towards the tent and got within earshot of the most vile and horrible language that I had ever heard. I realized that I would need more than my three stripes to give me the power that I needed to walk into that inferno. As I entered and looked around for the most likely person to make inquiries, I noticed that nobody was wearing their medals or badges of recognition. The screaming which seemed so unnecessary, seemed to be the best way to get anybody's attention.

Very gingerly I walked to a table where a young man sat typing. I stood next to him, practically against him to draw his attention. He stopped, looked up at me and asked what I wanted. The question was not asked very gentlemanly like, but I showed him my letter of authority to collect the Colonel that had come up by train from Cairo.

The young man asked whether I could see a train in the tent? Then asked if I could see any Colonel in the tent? This rude response to my question knocked all the wind out of my sails, and I left that tent like a dog that had been severely beaten. I was none the wiser than I was when I arrived there. But I looked around and in the distance spotted a train . . . an engine with five passenger coaches, five Red Cross coaches. About sixty other platform carriages were loaded with all kinds of armaments, trucks, carriers and guns. I gave a sigh of relief. At least I had located the train.

All I had to do now was to find the Colonel and tell him who I was and what my mission was.

I managed to drive my small truck in between guns, tents, trucks, planes and ammunition dumps. I decided to start from the engine and drive down close to the side of the train hoping that I could spot the new arrival. Unfortunately the new arrival spotted me first by recognizing the company sign painted on the door of the truck. I looked out of my cab into the face of a man that had practically gone berserk. He hollered, screamed, shouted, and waved his arms frantically in the air as he leaned out of the compartment window. I brought the small truck to a stop, jumped out of the cab and walked toward the carriage, and presented my new Colonel with one of the smartest salutes that I could possibly muster. As he gazed down at me with fiery eyes I could see that my salute and my appearance had enraged him even more.

"Is this what you have brought to fetch me and the Captain?" he screamed at me. I could not answer. I was too shocked. The camp Commandant had told me that there would be only one person to pick up, and now there were two. Together they both began to unload their baggage and I stood at the receiving end grabbing what came flying out of the compartment window. They then climbed down off the train.

The Colonel approached me first and looked at me as though I was something that had just been pulled out of a sewer. I tried the smart salute once again, but that didn't seem to have the effect that I thought it would. I heard him scream about the sunset and that it was getting dark.

The Captain then stood alongside the Colonel and what he saw did not please him either. The Captain managed to climb into the back while the Colonel managed to climb into the cab. In a very nasty way he told me to drive ten miles out of Benghazi where we would pull off the road for the night and bed down.

There was much traffic on the road and it was most difficult to drive in the dark. Usually one was able to move around by the moonlight, but it would be my luck that the very night that I needed old mister moon to help me, he was not there.

We pulled off alongside the busy, dusty, bumpy highway. As we climbed out the Captain instructed me to get busy and make coffee. I advised him that it was against the orders. He screamed back at me and told me just what he thought of such orders, and commanded me to make coffee with or without a fire. I made both the fire and the coffee. The last instruction that the Colonel hurled at me was, "Driver, see that we get on the road at 4:00 sharp!"

I did not sleep that night for fear that I might oversleep and fail to carry out the instructions of the not-so-happy Colonel, and the not-so-happy Captain. I lay on the hard ground under my blanket striking matches all night to see that my watch had not stopped.

The first thing the Colonel and his associate did when I awoke them at four a.m. sharp, was to shout for water that they might get shaved and cleaned up. The word shave sent a chill down my spine. It was practically a foreign word to me. I loaded the truck once again and we got back on the road towards Tripoli.

The tension had seemed to ease after the first few hours of driving, and then the Colonel bombarded me with questions about the officers and the men of his new command. He seemed to be a lot friendlier, but did not seem to appreciate the fact that I was Jewish. I had made a special point of letting him know this, but he seemed disinterested.

As we seemed to get on a friendly basis and I was beginning to relax somewhat the Colonel unexpectedly smashed his cane against the dashboard of the truck and screamed at me, "When last did you put a razor to that dirty face of yours?"

I could not answer because I was not sure. I apologized and assured him that the moment I got back to the camp I would find my razor and shave, and bathe. I also told him that I would let the other men in the camp know about his feelings. I hoped that this would take away some of the sting from me.

This was the longest journey that I have ever taken in my life. Sometimes I would wish that we would hit a land mine that I would be able to get rid of my two passengers in this way. At times I hoped that Gerrie would fly over and pay us an unexpected visit by blowing up the trucks in the area so that these shiny bright men from the base camp would get a little taste of what I had been through in the desert. We did stop once or twice along the road to have a snack, but I kept well out of the way in case they would find more fault with me.

It was practically sunset when I pulled off the road to drive out into the desert where our camp was situated. "Where do you think you are going now?" the Colonel asked. I told him that this was where the camp was situated. He again banged his cane on the dashboard. I knew that the place was not to his liking.

When we drove in between the tents he used some of his popular paraphrases again, and I knew that he intended making some big alterations. The other officers that came to welcome their new Colonel did not receive any better reception than what I did. I hastily unloaded the truck and got away to my tent as fast as I could. The other N. C. O's gathered around me trying to get a full report on the new officer commanding. In five minutes I had them all as defeated as I was personally. I let them know without a shadow of a doubt that we were all in for one big, big change.

It was strange to see the sudden change that had come upon every member of the company. There was no room at the wash basins to wash and to shave. Clean clothing was now being worn, and some of the men were even busy trying their best to clean their trucks and cars, while others were trying to get all the garbage out of their tents and bury it deep in the desert sand. It had been quite some time that we had heard the company trumpeter blow reveille in the morning, and it was obvious when it blew the next morning.

"I will see to it that this place will be changed and changed in a big hurry," the screaming Colonel aroused everybody as he marched away in a fit of temper hitting his cane vigorously against his leg.

It did not take very long to see a great change come over the camp and the personnel. I began to appreciate the new commanding officer and realized that we had drifted away from responsibility, from cleanliness and self-respect.

One day one of my buddies came rushing into the tent frantically waving a sheet of paper in his hand and at the same time yelling, "Home-leave, home-leave, I've got my home-leave." I jumped to my feet and snatched the paper that he was frantically waving in the air, and was surprised to read that he had been granted the opportunity to return to his home in South Africa. I heard other shouts from other tents and realized there were more men granted a home-leave. Some were laughing, some were crying, while others just stood there stunned.

Tears came into my eyes as I realized that I was not one of the fortunate ones. I had been away from home for four years at this time, and felt very strongly that I was also entitled to a spot of home-leave.

It was about two months later that I was jumping and shouting with my notification that I would be returning to my home in South Africa.

For me it was not a happy journey back to Cairo along the Mediterranean Ocean. It never did seem to be a lucky road for me. This time I developed a bad case of dysentery. Why it had to happen at this time I could not understand. At times when I'd scream for the driver to stop the men would simply hold me hanging out of the back of the truck. It was a hopeless condition to be in, but who worried about the condition when it meant going back home?

We did stop once again in Benghazi, and I inquired at one of the tents what I could do to stop this attack of dysentery. One cook advised me to drink much flour and water which would solidify my stomach. I drank it and it truly solidified my stomach. It took me days after to try to de-solidify my stomach.

At Cairo all the soldiers were issued the first medal given to the military forces of South Africa. We were all mighty proud of our "African Star."

We were herded like sheep aboard the Polish ship, *Kosciusko*. I was among those that were allocated to the bottom deck. It was so hot and stuffy down there that the first thing everyone did was to disrobe. The perspiration just streamed down the bodies of the men. It was only natural to make for the upper deck to get out into fresh air, but orders soon came through that nobody was allowed on the upper deck until sunset. Orders were orders, and every soldier understands that they are given and had to be obeyed.

In the evening everyone had taken his blanket to the upper deck and it was practically impossible to walk anywhere without standing on somebody. We did the best we could to reserve our places night after night. At sunrise we'd all make for the decks below. The very thought of returning home kept us from complaining more than what we did.

All day we would spend our time gambling with either dice or cards. Soon orders came, "Gambling will not be permitted, and home-leave will be cancelled." So the little entertainment we had found was forbidden, and to play "for fun" was not exciting.

Once or twice a day we had station calls and every man would grab his life-jacket and run to whatever deck had been allocated to him. We had been hearing bad news about many merchant ships that had been sunk along the African coast in the Indian Ocean. This was precisely where we were sailing, and we hoped that no German submarine would spot us. The action stations was a precaution to get as many lives saved as possible should we be torpedoed. It was not a very pleasant thought, but once again the thought of being back home overpowered the thought of being sunk by a German submarine.

One particular day there was much excitement amongst the crew. We could hear them shouting to one another in their Polish tongue, something about a German man-o-war. We looked through the portholes and in the distance we could see a big black ship. The *Kosciusko* was frantically signalling for them to identify themselves. But there was no response from that ship. Suddenly our ship turned left pointing the big Howitzer gun toward that big black ship on the horizon. Other than that nothing exciting transpired, that big black ship forced us to go well off our intended course. This might have been a blessing in disguise.

After twenty-one days we were thrilled to see land in the distance. We were told that in only a few hours we would be docking in Durban. The joy, thrill and excitement I felt as we pulled up alongside the dock was overpowering. Thousands of people stood there frantically waving Union Jack flags as well as South African flags. The gangplank was lowered and tears streamed down my eyes as I watched the first men to alight, kneel down and kiss the ground.

I walked down that gangplank so proud and happy that one would have thought I had won the war single-handed. We climbed aboard the trucks and were taken to a base camp on the coast. We were given final instructions and handed papers which would allow us to travel to our respective homes, and advised that we would receive a letter in the mail at a later date advising us of further procedures.

We were now free to go and do as we pleased. No more orders, no more commands, no more instructions and no more bosses. I was ready to "live it up."

Wherever I went I made sure that my medal could be seen.

So many congratulated me on being home and on my bright shining medal that hung on my chest. I managed to get aboard a troup train that was leaving Durban for my hometown Johannesburg. Like the ship it was well packed, but the thought once again of seeing my loved ones overpowered the thought of being uncomfortable.

All along the way we would stop and unload different soldiers and receive a rousing welcome at each place. Eventually the train steamed into the Johannesburg railway station, and I was the first to jump off even before it had stopped to run straight into the arms of my sister who stood there weeping. Then I embraced my dad and other members of the family, and many friends who had come to welcome me back home.

That night my dad had arranged a welcome-home dance for me in his hotel.

It was wonderful to feel once again being appreciated and wanted by people. I did my utmost to regulate my drinking (and smoking) as it had become a habit with me. Both in the front lines and in the base camp I had indulged rather vigorously, and I knew that I would now have to control the habit, if at all possible. I did not realize that I had been hooked—an alcoholic. At first it did not seem important to me, but suddenly when I found myself looking for the next one, I knew that somehow or other I would have to quit the habit. The very thought of it did not frighten me as I was sure that it would not be too difficult. Much to my surprise I found out that it was more difficult than what I had thought.

The dance was a great success and as my dad and I stood there embracing one another, both were intoxicated.

I wondered what the future held for me?

Chapter Three
From Sergeant to Director

Naturally it was a big, big change to what I had been accustomed to for the past four years. My father did all that he possibly could do to make me feel both comfortable and at ease. No doubt he could see how uncomfortable I was trying to adjust back into civilian life. "All will be well, my son," he tried to assure me as he placed his arm about me.

A few days later my father called me into his office and suggested that I become an interested partner in his hotel. I declined immediately telling him that I would have to consider the matter, as I was drinking very heavily. My father did his best to persuade me that my habit was nothing serious, and that I could quite easily overcome it. He wanted an immediate reply so I went into business with him as a shareholder.

It was utterly impossible for me to adapt myself to this new way of life. Not only was it difficult to get used to the civilian way of life, but I had never been in business before.

There was utter chaos in the city with regard to obtaining certain foods, and other necessities which had been strictly rationed. Butter was one of the main commodities used in the hotel restaurant, and was practically unobtainable. My father gave me a letter he had written to a young lady who worked in a grocery store. The name on the envelope read "Miss Van."

I drove downtown to the store, and down in the basement I was introduced to "Miss Van." She was beautiful. I must have looked stupid to her, as I stood there as though shocked at what stood before me. Her delightful laugh brought me back to reality.

"Can I help you sir?" she asked with such a sweet smile and a gentle laugh.

I said nothing, but just handed her the letter.

41

On opening the letter she smiled, and as she read it she laughed. Then she folded the letter and envelope and looked at me through the most beautiful blue eyes I had ever seen. With those eyes she examined me closely.

"So you are Harry Rubenstein's son who is back from the war?"

I had an idea that she liked what she saw. The only words that came to my mouth were, "Can I please take you out tonight?"

She laughed aloud and threw back her head as her long hair hung down her back. "I've only met you, my dear friend, this minute, and we hardly know each other, and you are already asking me to go out with you." With that she turned quickly to go to a refrigerator which stood in the corner of the store. On her return she handed me a parcel, and I paid her for the butter. "Give my love to your Dad, please," she said ever so sweetly.

She walked away and just left me standing there with my parcel of butter. I turned around with a heart filled with "Miss Van." I returned to the hotel to tell my Dad about this lovely lady who had served me in the store. My father said that he had forgotten to tell me to ask the young lady for small glasses which were also difficult to get at that time. This naturally gave me an excuse to return to the grocery store to see her.

This time I had decided that I would not leave the store until I had made a date with her. I was thrilled as she seemed to come rushing up to help me.

"How are you this morning Mr. Harry Rubenstein's soldier boy?" she laughingly asked me as she stretched out her hand to greet me.

I grabbed her hand as fast as I could and wanted to hang on to it forever. I explained about the drinking glasses that my father needed. She explained about the difficulty in getting the factory to send the type of glass we needed. Nevertheless, she gave me a few dozen glasses, and then I approached the dating subject. She did her best to avoid this, assuring me that she was "going steady." I asked if I could phone the following day. She seemed disinterested.

I phoned the following day, and the following day, and

42

the following day. Each phone call assured me that the young lady was not interested in the returned soldier, but I persisted.

I decided to stand outside that store one day and wait until "Miss Van" would vacate the premises. As she left the store and walked along the sidewalk I joined her. I made as though it was an accidental meeting, but she knew otherwise. She decided to put my mind at ease by accepting an invitation to dinner the following evening. I could hardly believe the acceptance.

My dad suggested that he take me to the rest of the family, and they would be able to introduce me to some nice "Yiddisha girl." This I did and I met some very, very nice yiddisha girls. But that young lady in the grocery store that had supplied the butter and the drinking glasses, had me well and truly hooked. And there was no way possible that I could see to get myself unhooked.

One evening I took a young lady out to a cabaret and as we sat at the side of the dance floor speaking, much to my surprise the "butter lady" was sitting across from us. I tried to attract her attention one way or another but failed. Apparently she wanted to avoid me. The following morning I phoned to let her know that I had seen her the previous evening, and much to my surprise she asked me to meet her after work.

My knees practically buckled under me at this invitation. Needless to say I was there two hours before the time. As she left the store and walked along the sidewalk I rushed across the road from where I was standing and practically got killed by a speeding car. I walked up to her, took her by the hand, and much to my surprise and happiness, she closed her hand around mine and held it tightly.

As we walked hand in hand she explained that she had heard that I was going to be at the cabaret the previous evening and had made it her business to be there so that she could see me.

For seven years we walked hand in hand. I decided one evening to let my father know that I was going to marry the girl that he had introduced me to by the way of butter and drinking glasses. My father said that he had expected this, but

43

would rather that I had married one of the other Jewish girls that I had met.

On my birthday the lady who sold the butter, and the drinking glasses, the lady called "Miss Van," became my wife.

We had acquired a beautiful furnished apartment on the roof of the new hotel that my father and I had now bought.

My father and I had decided that now that we were partners we could go into a bigger business. This new hotel did practically ten times the business of the other one, and belonged to my uncle who wanted to sell it. It was situated in the center of many sports fields and directly across the road from the Turffontein Horse Racing Track.

I was now discharged from the army and was caught up with all forms of gambling, the main one being horse-racing. My wife had also adopted the gambling spirit, and lived with a deck of cards in her hands practically day and night.

One evening my father sent a message to me that he would like to see me in his office. As I walked into the office I noticed how pale my father was and terribly annoyed. I sat down and in a gentle voice asked, "What is the matter Dad?" In no small way did my father tell me how much I had embarrassed him. How disgracefully I had been behaving. He finally ended his scolding by asking me to leave the hotel at my earliest convenience. I felt sorry for my father as I had never seen him in such a state of mind. I knew that what he had said about my drinking, fighting and bad behaviour were all true. I promised to leave as soon as possible, and he said that he would pay me my portion immediately.

I explained the situation to my wife, and she fully agreed with my father whom she loved very, very much.

I managed to buy a hotel of my own in Kimberly, South Africa. Kimberly is one of the biggest diamond-producing cities in the world. The Kimberly diamond mines are well-known throughout the entire world. DeBeers diamond mines are the biggest in South Africa. It was known as THE KILLARNEY HOTEL, but I changed the name to the WEST END HOTEL. It had off sales departments, as well as bars, lounges, restaurants, dance floors and cabarets. Business was more than I could think it would ever be. Money kept coming in by the barrel-load. All departments were flourishing. This caused my little heart to be overjoyed. It also caused my wife's heart to be overjoyed.

The lounges and dance floors were most attractive, particularly to the younger groups. There were many birthday parties given in the restaurant by young people. It was the law of the country that nobody under the age of eighteen was permitted to be supplied with alcohol. At times I would notice birthday parties would have young girls and boys under the age of eighteen. I had no scruples as far as making money was concerned.

There was such a demand for the things of the world by my customers that I felt obliged to build a house of prostitution alongside my hotel. Unbeknown to my wife or family, the business started to flourish and the best customers were the rich men of the city. I would furnish the necessary entertainment as well as the necessary liquor which would cost me approximately fifteen pounds ($7). I would ask fantastic prices for such entertainment that I had to furnish.

Money. Money. Money. This had become my god.

On a certain day a diamond cutter walked into my bar with a few friends who began drinking very heavily. By evening time they were over-intoxicated. As they left the bar, shouting farewells and laughing and shouting, the diamond cutter stretched forth his hand to shake hands with me, and as I shook hands with him I felt something cold in the palm of my hand. He closed my hand over that cold thing and walked out of the bar. I held my arm under the bar counter and was shocked to see a small glass bottle filled with cut diamonds.

I immediately left the bar and went into my office, locking the door so that nobody would see me examining the gift that was given to me. For the first time in my life I had made contact with diamonds. As I rolled thirteen stones from one hand to the other, the twinkling of the diamonds began to fascinate me.

One of my first warnings I had received from friends upon entering into business in Kimberly was to make sure that I never got involved with diamond smuggling. But here it was, as simple as this, what was there to fear? For hours I sat in my office toying with those beautiful stones and wondered what they were worth.

Early the following morning I received a telephone call from the man that had left the diamonds. He asked me to bring the "gift" to his house that he had left with me the previous night. He was cautious not to mention the word *diamond*, as this was a dangerous word to use in the city of Kimberly. Practically every day the police arrested somebody that was trying to get rich through illicit diamond deals. I asked the caller on the telephone what parcel, or what gift he was referring to? (I did not think that he was in a condition to remember that he had left the diamonds with me.) He cautioned me not to try and be clever, but to get the gift over to his place immediately, otherwise he would be obliged to come and fetch it himself with a gun.

In no way did I want to get involved with diamonds and gunslingers, so I took the bottle with the thirteen stones inside, drove to his house, and unloaded the pretty little gift. My friend explained that there was much money to be made in dealing with the polished stones that he could give me, and it was legal to deal with polished diamonds. "The ones that get you into serious trouble," he said, "are the rough diamonds that are uncut." He came back to the hotel with me and we discussed the diamond business. My wife walked in on the discussion and he asked her to hold out her hand while he poured the thirteen stones into her hand. She was amazed at the beauty. I asked the man what he would want for that bottle of diamonds. He gave me a figure, as well as a list of the carats per stone.

I made a special trip by train to see whether I could find any connections in the large city of Johannesburg. It did not take me long to find the people I was looking for. I showed them the list of what I could get for them and they made me an offer without even seeing the stones. The offer was well above the price that the owner of the diamonds asked for. This excited me to see the immense profit that I could personally make on the stones. I hurried back to inform my friend that I had buyers for the stones.

I wanted to become popular in the city and get to know the wealthy people that were worth knowing. Especially those associated with the diamond mines. There were quite a number of them in the Freemason's Lodges, so I made it my business to attend many lodge meetings. Freemasonry was entertaining and I did meet some very influential people. Occasionally I would have a big ball for the Freemasons and this gave me much popularity. I also met a few men who worked in the DeBeer's diamond mine and we'd discuss diamonds. They explained how easy it was for them to bring the uncut stones out of the mines if they had somebody to sell the stuff for them. The uncut stone could be seen in the face of the wall in the mine and they merely dug it out with a pocketknife. When I told them that it would be simple for me to dispose of uncut stones, a slow, but steady, supply began arriving.

I was informed by people who had seen my business more than triple itself that there was another very easy and simple way to make my banking account swell beyond recognition. They told of a certain area near the gold mines that accommodated thousands of mine workers who were unable to obtain any alcoholic beverage. Firstly because they were restricted by law and secondly because it was unobtainable. I was informed that these thousands of people would pay any price to get possession of brandy. A bottle of brandy at that time was costing me seven shillings and sixpence ($1), and I was told that I could get between eight and ten dollars a bottle.

This fantastic profit got me over interested, and I worked out a scheme whereby I could send truckloads of brandy into the area. One truck would carry two hundred cases of brandy, with a dozen bottles a case. The profit was immense. I was unable to deposit the money in the bank in case the Revenue Services might inquire when and how the money was made. So I kept bundles and bundles of notes stored in my clothing closet. My wife had no idea about my illegal diamond deal, neither did she have any idea about my illicit liquor deal. She was too busy dealing cards.

Early one morning I was paid an unexpected visit by the chief of police. He was most friendly, and this kind of troubled me, because on other occasions he was rude to me. He told me that the police had found a large truck in the gold mining area with two hundred cases of brandy inside. They had also uncovered a very large hole which had been dug in the ground that too had been filled with cases of brandy. I asked him why he had come to see me about this find? He told me that I was well acquainted with the liquor dealers in the city and the surrounding areas, and that he would appreciate it very much if I would notify the police authorities should I hear of anybody who would have done such a terrible thing. I promised him faithfully that I would work in close corroboration with the police, and if anything suspicious might arise I would not hesitate to call him personally and notify him. We then sat together drinking and discussing the city of Kimberly in general. Somehow I could detect a note of sarcasm in his voice, and as he stood to shake hands and bid me farewell I was sure that I saw a sneer upon his face.

I walked back into the hotel and told my wife that it was important that I visited a friend of mine down in Riverton.

This was a small town about twenty miles away from the hotel, and was situated on the river. I had a man working there for me and his duties were to wash labels off the brandy bottles, and remove any names from the cases. This was a precaution, in case the police might find the stuff, they would not be able to trace the supplier. That was my philosophy.

My wife accompanied me not knowing why I had suddenly decided to take a ride down to the river. I called my friend while my wife visited his wife, and asked him what kind of supply he still had hidden in his house. He said that there were approximately one thousand cases of brandy still there ready to be loaded. I told him about the visit from the chief-of-police, and that it was now most important for us to get rid of any evidence that there might be. We immediately began loading the truck and once we had filled it we proceeded towards the river.

The shock of what had happened in the last few hours had affected my mind to a large extent. I suggested that we drive the truck with all the brandy cargo right into the river and that would be a good action which would immediately hide all evidence. The other fellow disagreed very forcibly and mentioned the stupidity in losing the truck as well as the brandy. We therefore parked alongside the river and began throwing the evidence into the water. I was most unhappy that we were unable to throw the evidence deeper into the river so I suggested to my friend that he strip and jump into the river, and then I would hand him cases of brandy so that he could carry them deeper into the water. It was a winters morning and he suggested that I strip and step into the river. I felt that there was no time to debate or argue about who was going to get into the river, so we remained on the bank and threw case after case and bottle after bottle as far as we possibly could out into the water.

I noticed that there were a group of fishermen sitting about a hundred and fifty feet away. They looked like fishermen because they were dressed like fishermen, and had sticks between their legs and appeared to be waiting to make a catch. Unbeknown to me I was the catch that they were waiting to make.

We had practically unloaded the evidence when suddenly the fishermen jumped up, ran along the bank of the river towards us brandishing revolvers high in the air and screaming, "If you run, Mr. Rubenstein, we will shoot you."

As they surrounded me I looked at my friend the chief of police that had been with me in the hotel and said, "Where on earth do you think I'm going to run to?" The police placed my employee and myself under arrest, and all the shouting and excitement had brought my wife and my friends wife to the scene of the crime. I quickly explained to my startled wife what I had been doing and how I had been caught and what had happened in the gold mining area.

I was a wealthy man with one of the most prosperous and progressive businesses in the city, and for the life of me I could not understand why I had done these ridiculous and stupid things. I explained to my attorney what had taken place and he assured me that there was nothing to worry about. He arranged with the chief to let me go on my own recognizance, and I was glad to walk out of the company of policemen.

My attorney advised me to obtain the services of a very good friend of his, a lawyer, which I did. The lawyer in turn advised me to get the services of a very good friend of his who was an advocate, which I did. I was desperate and nobody knew it better than these three men. Regardless of what the cost would be I hated to think that I would subsequently be placed behind bars.

The initial evidence at the trial was very weak and my three friends, the lawyer, the advocate, the attorney, were sure that the police had no legitimate case against me. This was most encouraging, but what I did not know was that the chief witness was unable to be found. My attorney had bribed him to stay in one of the rooms in his office until the case was over. But somebody had spotted the chief witness going into the building and had reported it to the police, who wasted no time in getting this chief witness to give evidence. Once he started it seemed that he would continue for a lifetime. Even the judge found it very difficult to stop him. If ever anybody enjoyed giving evidence in a court case, that man enjoyed giving evidence against me. Other evidence was brought forward and twenty-eight charges were brought against me. The judge brought the case to a sudden close.

The following morning my advocate put forward a plea of mercy and told the judge how I had contemplated running for mayor of the city of Kimberly. He also mentioned very strongly that I was a good member of the Freemasons. I was later told that the judge was also a very good member of the Freemasons, and that was probably the reason that I was not sent to jail.

I was given a very heavy fine but I had the money to pay it. There were other very high expenses attached to the case such as my advocate, attorney and lawyer. But I had the money to pay them too.

The great shock came when the judge pronounced me as an unfit liquor licensee, and stated that whatever other licenses I might have, be immediately taken away from me.

My wife and I examined our banking account and found

that we still had quite a substantial amount which would help us to move to another city. While we were still contemplating the move and the payment thereof I was paid an unexpected visit by the Internal Revenue Service. He closely examined the records and the books that had been returned by the police and proved that my returns that I had been sending in year after year were incorrect. I told him that I was willing to pay whatever amount he thought I owed, and this saved me once again from appearing in court on a charge of falsification of record.

After paying what the revenue authorities thought to be the outstanding amount I found myself penniless. It was most difficult to accept the situation I now found myself in. A man who had put thousands of dollars on one race horse. A man who had handled thousands of dollars worth of diamonds. A man who had handled much cash. Now that man finds himself penniless.

I now managed to move back to Johannesburg and soon found a job as a commercial traveler. The difficulty was to find a suitable car to travel around in. I went to a Freemason friend of mine who ran a secondhand car business. He had heard about my turmoil and suggested giving me a car to be paid for as best I could. I appreciated his thoughtfulness and took the car that he offered. I then started traveling around the country selling tables and chairs, as well as Steel American kitchen cupboards to the furniture dealers.

The shock of having to battle to make money was not pleasant at all. I carried on as best I could to keep house and home together, but could in no way overcome the tragedy that had taken place in my life. I paid my father a visit and he wept as he told me that he had read the full account of my court case in the local newspapers. He said that he was amazed to see that his son would stoop to such a low level in order to become rich. I knew that the remainder of the family felt exactly the same way about what I had done, so I did not make any effort to visit them.

There were times that I would accidentally bump into an acquaintance. Some would sympathize with me over my great business loss, while others would say "Better luck next

time, Hymie," and walk off laughing loudly. I failed to see
the humor of the whole thing. At times when I would recall
the day that the Judge sat in his large high leather-bound
black chair and peered over his glasses at me . . . I sat next
to my attorney . . . he said, "I now proclaim judgment,"
and the police officer shouted, "Rubenstein, stand to your
feet." The Public Prosecutor shouted, "Your worship, this
man must be sentenced to four years imprisonment."

My attorney shouted, "This man is innocent until
proven guilty," and the perspiration kept running down my
legs into my shoes, cold chills would run up and down my
spine. I would recall the times that the court would be in
session and I would see myself standing behind prison bars
in a convict's uniform.

The court case was over but the memory lingered on.

Chapter Four
From Suicide to Salvation

I now had three daughters at the Jr. School, a wife to take care of, as well as a house rental to pay, and an unpaid car.

As I rode from city to city trying to sell my wares I resorted once again to heavy drinking. I could no longer afford the expensive whiskey drinks I used to enjoy, so I resorted to cheap wine. In the early morning before the bars opened I would be hanging around waiting to have my first drink for the day, hoping that this would have a tendency to steady my already unsteady nerves.

I discovered that my wares were not popular, and neither was I.

On my thirty-seventh birthday in a small town called Bothasville I invited in a few friends. We celebrated the birthday as best we could drinking out of jars of cheap wine.

I woke up the next morning amazed at the mess that my room was in. The stench nauseated me. I opened all the doors and windows in the room and could not understand how a human being could find himself in such a filthy, stinking pigsty.

I paced up and down the corridor deciding that before the maid would come to clean my room I had better do some cleaning myself. I wrapped a handkerchief over my nose and mouth and did the best I could with wet towels to clean the mess around the bed and cupboards. Cigar and cigarette stubs were lying everywhere, and in places had burned holes in the hotel carpeting.

I packed my clothing and left the hotel before there were any complaints about my room.

I went into the bar of some other hotel to try once again to steady my unsteadied mind. As I sat in the bar looking in the mirror in front of me trying to find some way out of my dilemma I saw a way to commit suicide. It flashed into my mind so quickly I was amazed at the simplicity of the whole thing. I was amazed that I had not thought of this "easy way out" before. I saw myself driving down into the valley which was alongside the town at a very high speed. The car I was driving was capable of doing 100 mph. I saw the bridge down in the valley. It was a large concrete and steel bridge spanning the river. I turned the steering wheel very slightly and the car careered off the road into the bridge and I was instantly killed. To kill myself seemed to be very easy, and nobody would ever think that it was suicidal, but that I had lost control of the car.

With this plan there would be no further worry for me, no further troubles for me, and no further responsibility. My wife would also benefit by this as the insurance company would most certainly pay her the claim.

This was the birthday present I was going to give myself.

On the way to doing what I had now planned to do I decided to call on my friend (who had arranged with me to have the party in the hotel room) to tell him that I would see him in hell. I had no doubt that I was hell-bound, and I had no doubt that he was heading for the same place.

I drove to his place of business, a furniture store on the outskirts of the city. I noticed his car was not there but that the doors were open.

I walked through the furniture store and entered into the office where a young lady was sitting behind the office desk, speaking on the telephone. I sat down and waited for her to finish. As she replaced the receiver she smiled at me and asked if she could be of any help. I asked for my friend, the manager. She informed me that he had left for the day to buy furniture from some factory. In a way I was disappointed that I could not give my friend the message that I wanted to give him.

As I stood to lift my case and leave, the young lady asked me not to leave.

"What is it that you want young lady?" I asked, thinking that she was probably of the similar type that had been in my hotel room the night before.

She looked straight into my eyes, lifted her arm and

pointed her finger directly at me, then said, "Brother, Jesus showed me that you are a very troubled and worried man."

I thought my heart would stand still when I heard her make this announcement and mention the name of Jesus. In a split second I recalled all the embarrassment and trouble that this man had caused me, and now this young lady (who I believed could be nothing else but a bad mental case) was telling me about this Jesus. I was enraged.

I screamed and yelled and repeated my name over and over assuring her that I was a young God-fearing Jewish man who knew her Jesus to be nothing but an imposter, an illegitimate child and a deceiver.

Much to my surprise, my wild fits had no effect on her at all. I doubt very much she heard one word I had said. She remained so composed and so at ease it caused me to become even more threatening than at first. I realized what the consequences would be if I would strangle her—having just recently faced a judge, and had no intention of facing another.

Quickly I walked out of the store cursing and blaspheming and using whatever obscene language I knew, hoping that something I would say would deeply hurt the young lady who had mentioned the name of Jesus to me.

I took the keys of my car out of my pocket, and as I placed it into the door a strange thing happened. I suddenly got the most painful craving for tea. I did not understand this at all, for I was not a tea drinker. What on earth did I want tea for? I knew nothing about tea. I did not know that tea came from China, I did not know about the Boston Tea Party, and I hardly knew how to spell the word. But here I was craving for tea.

I felt very badly about the insult that that young lady had given me as a Jewish man. I decided to go back and give myself the satisfaction that I had hurt her in some way before driving away, also hoping to find tea.

Whatever ego I had had that young lady had destroyed it with the announcement that she had made to me about Jesus. I intended fully restoring my ego by once again becoming the great big Rubenstein.

As I reentered the store, much to my surprise the lady

was standing a few feet behind me. The question she asked me even before I could say anything baffled me completely. "Don't you perhaps feel like a nice cup of tea, Brother?" She had such a happy smile on her face.

For a time I just stood there stunned not knowing what to do, to say, or where to go. I said to her in no uncertain way, "Listen, young lady, you have annoyed and embarrassed me immensely by what you said to me in your office. I am really dying for a cup of tea, but I don't want any of this Jesus business."

She ushered me back into the office, and I watched her as she prepared the tea. As I sat there drinking the tea she offered me some nice-looking cookies, which I thoroughly enjoyed.

After a while she said, "Brother, do you mind if I read my Bible?" I made a sign to show her that I was not interested in what she was wanting to do, and continued sipping at my second cup of tea. She read aloud portions of both the Old and the New Testament. I did not understand what she was reading about. She then closed the Bible, laid it on the desk near her and suggested that I allow her to phone her pastor to come and pray for me.

"What on earth is a pastor?" I asked. I had never heard of anybody praying for anybody else, and had never heard of a pastor.

She seemed happy to tell me something that I had not heard before. "A pastor is a minister of God, and I am sure that you will like my pastor when he comes to speak, and to pray for you."

I had no doubt that the lady was a bad mental case. First she told me that Jesus had showed her I was a worried man, and now she wants somebody to come and pray for me.

I sat there as she phoned for the pastor, but the man was not at home as she expected. She showed no signs of disappointment but immediately suggested that she take me to meet an old friend of hers.

"Who is this friend of yours?" I asked.

"It is an old lady friend of mine who is now eighty years of age and she will be such a blessing to you as she prays for you," she assured me.

I began quickly to scheme a way to upset the lady and break down her line of attack in getting somebody to pray for me. I noticed quite a few customers had come into the store and were crowding around. Some had probably come with the full intentions of buying. I thought I would confuse the lady so I said, "If you will go with me right away to see your lady friend of eighty, I would go now but not later."

She jumped up delighted and ran into the furniture store asking everybody to leave immediately, and if possible to return later. Apparently at this moment the last thing in the lady's mind was to sell furniture and to make money. My plan failed drastically and the action which she had so quickly taken left me dumbfounded.

She ran back into the office and was so happy that she was now able to take me to go and find her friend.

"What about the customers that you have chased away?" I asked.

She failed to give me a reply, but took me hastily by the arm and ushered me out of the store, locking all the doors behind her.

We climbed into my car and she directed me to the house of her elderly friend.

I knocked on the door and the servant answered.

"Where is the old girl?" I asked her.

"Early this morning the Madame climbed up the mountain to go and pray," she said as she pointed in the direction where I had parked the car. I noted a half mile further was a mountain about 600 feet high.

I became fearful realizing that I had allowed myself to get involved with mentally-sick people. The lady who had come with me was now standing there hand in hand with the servant. They seemed so happy as they stood there talking about things I had never heard of. The servant seemed just like the young lady—as though a fire was burning in her bones.

I decided before I met any more of these mentally-disturbed people I had better run for my life. I ran as quickly as I could through the garden, out of the gate and got to my car once again. I was annoyed that I had locked the doors because now it would hinder my getaway. I was trembling and could not control the bunch of keys I held in my hand. I gazed at them as I stood there shaking and failed to recognize the ignition key which would unlock my door. The third key I tried unlatched the door and I jumped in and slammed the door behind me. Once again I tried to find the key to start the car and had the same trouble inside the car as I had outside the car.

I panicked when I saw the lady come through the garden and out the gate. She tried the door of the car on her side, but it was locked and I signalled her to get away. She ran around the front of the car to my side and opened the door, and said in such a sweet voice, "Please, Brother, be so kind as to take me home."

I opened the back door and she climbed in. She then directed me to her house where I stopped and told her to get out quickly.

"Brother, I feel so unworthy to pray for you," she said, "because I have only been saved five weeks, but I would very much like to."

For the moment I wondered what she was referring to. I thought that she might have fallen in a well, or a river, or something, and somebody had saved her. I turned around in disgust and said, "For heaven's sake, hurry up and pray for me and get out."

To my surprise the lady did not pray for me but jumped out of the car and ran into her house. I sat there wondering why she had done that after all the trouble she had gone to to find somebody to pray for me. Now that I had volunteered for her to pray for me, she had run away.

I decided to go and see what had happened to her and walked into the house to see what her trouble was. I walked into the living room and found her on her knees at the davenport. This annoyed me so I turned to leave.

"Please don't leave, Brother, I wish for you just to kneel at the other end of the davenport, so that I might be able to pray for you," she said, smiling up at me.

I looked at her and then looked at the spot that she had motioned me to kneel. It flashed through my mind that this was not an expensive item, and that it was actually not costing me any money at all. I kneeled where she had told me to kneel.

Much to my horror I heard her say, "Jesus, thou Son of David, save this Jewish man's soul." I felt that I was about to have a heart attack. I looked towards the lady. She had bowed her head and her arms were high up toward the sky and she was praying louder, and more earnestly than I believed anybody could pray. I thought that she would quit after five minutes. The first five minutes went by, and so did the second and third. After thirty minutes she was weeping. Suddenly she began laughing frantically. She then began to speak in a strange language which sounded like Italian. Then another that sounded like Egyptian. Then another that sounded like French. Then another that sounded like Chinese. I had never before heard the League of Nations come out of one mouth as it did out of the mouth of that young lady.

Her arms were now waving frantically in the air, and her hair was hanging down in her face, she was shaking her head from side to side while her body seemed to be shivering as if it had been chilled. I thought the lady had become hysterical.

I looked at her and had no doubt in my mind that she was now in shock, or in a bad coma. I decided to get close enough to her and punch her hard with my fist and thereby get her out of the coma that she had gotten herself into.

I raised my arm to give her a hard blow in the mouth. I got the fright of my life when my arm stuck up in the air and refused to come down. I spoke to my fist and said, "Come on fist, let us smash her and get out of here." My fist refused to respond.

The lady continued with her frightening actions and screams. I got madder than ever now that I was paralyzed in my right arm. I decided that probably I had got a cramp in the arm, so I felt if the rest of my body was still alive. Sure enough, my legs were in perfect shape. I decided to use the right leg and kick the lady viciously in the side. With my arm in the air, I lifted my leg, and was shocked that it stayed in the air with my right arm.

The lady ceased to perform and life came back into my body. I felt that something had taken place in my life because I seemed to be drawn to her. For the first time I recognized that she was totally different from others that I had associated with. Even her voice was different, and her behavior as well.

"Brother, it is your turn now to pray," she said to me ever so sweetly.

I felt terribly embarrassed because I did not know how to pray. I remembered the times that the so-called Christians had chased me out of their Bible study class and that at the commencement of every class they had said the Lord's Prayer. I decided to try and say that.

"Our Father, which art in heaven, hallowed be thy name," I started to say.

"No, Brother, you don't pray like that," the lady said.

I looked at her, and was aware that I was afraid of her, but she seemed to have a shine about her, and an authority about her that I had not seen before. I was no longer the big mighty mouse, but felt even less powerful than a small mini mouse.

"What do you want me to do?" I asked softly and meekly.

"Look up and tell Jesus that you accept Him as your personal Lord and Saviour and Master," she commanded.

Surely she was unaware of the consequences that I would have to undergo if I would ever dare to do what she had commanded me to do. I did appreciate the fact that I must do all that I possibly could do to avoid upsetting her in any way. After all, she had spent much time, and gone through much trouble to get me where she had me. I thought of the predicament I would be in if my father, or brother, or my sister would find me here with a young lady talking about the one we believed to be an imposter: Jesus. I decided not to upset her in any form as she seemed so genuine about her belief.

I sought to give her the impression that I was doing exactly what she had asked me to do. To make it more dramatic I threw my arms up into the air, thinking this would meet with her approval.

I then lifted my head and looked up. When I opened my eyes the greatest thing in my life took place. Little did

I know that the Great Creator of heaven and earth was waiting there in the portals of heaven, looking down on me, and waiting for me to look up at Him.

There was nobody better equipped than Almighty God himself to supply me with what I needed so desperately. He knew my circumstances, He knew my bad intentions, and He knew that what I needed more than anything in the world was His Son Christ Jesus of Nazareth.

I felt as though a large warm cushion was suddenly placed against my left side. I leaned toward it. It was so soft and felt so exceptionally warm. Then another similar pillow was placed against my back, then I felt another at my front, then I felt as though I was standing on yet another one, and then one seemed to be placed over me, and one on my right side, and I stood completely wrapped in the most indescribable peace, love and joy. All at once all these so-called "pillows" seemed to come inside of me. I felt, and I *knew* that I had been changed.

I looked toward the young lady hoping that she could explain this thrilling, gorgeous, and cleansing business that had taken place. I knew that she knew that I had been changed. All she could shout was, "Praise the Lord! Praise the Lord! Praise the Lord!"

For the first time I knew what it was to be *clean*. For the first time I knew what it was to be *free*. For the first time I knew what it was to be happy, and satisfied, and sanctified.

"How do you feel now my very dear brother?" the lady asked me as tears streamed down our faces.

I did not know what to say or do, but I took her by her hands, and weeping and laughing both at the same time I managed to blurt out, "My dear sister, I have never ever felt better."

We decided to go to a nearby restaurant as I told her that I was terribly hungry. As we walked out of the house I looked up into my wonderful God's heaven, and for the first time realized that He had put it there, and that He had made it blue. I looked at the green grass, and knew that God had placed it there. I looked at the beautiful green trees that lined the sidewalk, and as they swayed gently in the breeze

I knew that my God had sent the breeze and made the trees. I looked at the beautiful assorted plants and flowers in the garden and knew that God had made the flowers to open and had made the busy bees to buzz around and make honey from the pollen they were taking from those flowers. It was just too wonderful now to be alive. I felt like screaming and shouting and running around the streets telling everybody about this wonderful transformation that had taken place in my life. I looked at my car that had been parked in front of the house, and said to my friend, "That sure is a beautiful car, sister."

"That is your car, Brother!" she replied.

I knew without a shadow of a doubt that the Hymie Rubenstein that had gone into that house was not the same Hymie Rubenstein that had come out of it. All things had become new.

As we walked into the restaurant I looked around and noticed many travelers were there; some with pipes, some with cigarettes, and others with large cigars. "How can they put that filthy smoke into the temple of God?" I said to myself. I was a very heavy cigarette smoker myself, smoking between fifty to seventy-five cigarettes a day. I no longer had a desire to ever smoke again.

I lost the desire to do anything that would not be pleasing to this great big wonderful God. The moment He forgave me He set me free from all sin, iniquity and worldliness (and who the Son makes free is free indeed).

The following morning before sunrise I climbed out of my bed the happiest man in the world. Problems had left me. Worries had left me. Fear had left me, and no more did I want to kill myself but now I wanted to live that others might know and live as well.

I was so excited about paying the "pastor" a visit that first morning of my first day in Christ Jesus, that I forgot to have breakfast before leaving the hotel.

I knocked on the door of the pastor's house and a most charming middle-aged man stood in the doorway smiling. Before I could introduce myself he threw his arms around me, kissed me on both cheeks and forehead, and with tears running down his face he cried, "My new Jewish brother, welcome to my humble abode."

He excitedly ushered me into the living room as though he had found a most precious jewel and ran to fetch his wife. His wife did not walk from her bedroom to the living room, she ran. The three of us now stood with our hands in the air thanking God that another sinner had come out of the darkness into His wonderful light.

It was something entirely new to me to be standing with my arms in the air, weeping. We stood there for thirty minutes telling our most high and wonderful God that we appreciated Him. We sat down to relax and the pastor's wife busied herself preparing our breakfast.

I loved that praying business so much, I asked the pastor if we could kneel and pray a while. He was pleased to join me. A little later we enjoyed a lovely breakfast. After this the pastor read many portions of Scripture. I was thrilled and overjoyed with each Scripture that he read, for I not only understood it, but I knew that it had been written for me personally. An hour and thirty minutes had slipped away so quickly. "Do you mind Pastor Kruger if we get back on our knees again?" I asked my new friend.

Without replying he fell to his knees also. For the rest of the day we studied the Bible, we prayed, and we wept unashamedly before our King of Glory. We were so wrapped up in the love of God that we forgot everything else about us.

Suddenly the pastor cried out, "I have completely forgotten the service that I have to attend tonight in a church nearby. I want you to come along with me Brother Hymie. I am sure the congregation will be thrilled to meet their new converted Jewish brother," he said.

"Where is this church, pastor?" I asked.

He explained that the church had invited him, and that it was about twenty miles outside of Bothasville.

"I am sorry pastor that I cannot possibly accompany you," I said.

He looked at me inquiringly. "Why not, my dear brother? I would be most privileged to take you there and bring you back again," he said.

I explained that I had no intention of ever leaving the city of Bothasville. "This is where I met this wonderful Jesus that has done such a wonderful and amazing thing in my life. This is where I fully intend staying for the rest of my life."

He hastened to console my by telling me that the Son of God, the Lord Jesus Christ was everywhere, and if people all over the nation, and all over the world only seek for Him they would truly find Him. He also said that if they would call upon Him, He would most surely answer them.

"Will He be in that church of yours tonight?" I asked.

He laughed as he assured me that He would most certainly be there. With that assurance I told him that I would accompany him.

The twenty-mile journey seemed so short as we spoke only about the Lamb of God who takes away the sins of the world. We parked the car directly in front of the church and my window was turned down. I could hear loud music being played inside the building. I could see many people seated inside the church and on a platform, I could also see musicians who were playing many assorted types of instruments. I explained to the pastor that I would park the car and then join him inside the church. I intended to make a quick getaway as I felt that this was nothing but a rock and roll session.

Later I did find out that it was a rock and roll session, but this was a different type. (This was a Holy Spirit-filled Rock and Roll session. They were able to accomplish a most wonderful and rewarding fete. They got my Jewish feet on the Rock and Jewish name on the Roll.)

Apparently I began to find fault with everyone and everything in the place. To add to my fault-finding list the preacher began waving his arms in the air, jumping and running to and fro on the platform. My pastor friend who was sitting in the seat next to me jumped to his feet and ran toward the platform motioning to the preacher to come to him. The preacher fell down on his knees on the platform to listen to what my pastor friend had to say. He jumped up and this time shouted even louder, and waved his arms more frantically and made an announcement.

"Ladies and gentlemen, brethren, sisters and friends, visitors and members of this congregation, I have the most wonderful, thrilling, and exciting news that I have ever been able to tell this congregation. Sitting here tonight in our midst is a Son of Abraham. A young Jewish man who has accepted his Messiah Jesus Christ as his personal Lord and Saviour! Right here in our city he met the Master. Let us give him a most hearty Christian welcome."

The noise, the hand clapping, the shouting and praising God and the jumping and dancing that took place after that announcement frightened me.

There were many hard slaps on my back and shoulders as some of the people congratulated me. There were also very many handshakes, embraces, and kisses. I was not only frightened but felt most uncomfortable. This seemed to last for an eternity, and I was only hoping that it would cease.

When it appeared that everybody had now settled down (and I was glad that they had settled down) a lady sitting directly behind me jumped up and spoke in a language which I did not understand. This had a tendency to unsettle me. Somebody in another part of the church seemed to shout back to the one that had spoken those strange words. This time the language was English and I could understand a little of what was being said.

Then in another part of the building I heard another person speaking in a strange language which sounded very much as though it could have been Chinese. This was most strange to me, and although many strange things were happening, I wondered just how much more of these strange experiences I would experience?

Again, somebody else shouted back at that "Chinese" speaker and this time again in the English language. Now the whole congregation began clapping their hands. I saw some of the people watching me so I thought it would be better to act in the same manner. I clapped my hands very weakly, and felt like such a hypocrite.

I looked around and noticed at my left the sign "EXIT." I felt very strongly that before I got too involved with these strangely-behaved people I would be doing myself a favor by making an exodus through the door with the "EXIT" sign.

The pastor inquired if there were any sick people in

the congregation and invited them to come and stand in the front of the pulpit. At least 120 people walked to the front. Most of them had their hands in the air praising God. Others were weeping. I looked at the "EXIT" sign again, and had made up my mind that such a service and such behavior "was for the birds."

To my surprise my pastor friend joined the preacher and together they began praying for the people and laying hands on them. I noticed my pastor friend was holding a bottle of oil and putting it on the people. To my amazement a number of the people fell to the floor, and those that were in front of me fell too.

The preacher cried out, "Let every head be bowed and let every eye be closed."

As I looked around and saw that everybody was standing most reverently with their heads bowed and their eyes closed I decided that this was the most opportune time to make my getaway.

I moved to go but my feet seemed to be rooted to the ground. I looked at my feet and said, "Come on feet, let's get out of this place, and let's get out of here right now." I moved for the second time but my body only moved from the waist upwards, my feet refused to move. I tried once again but with no success. I could only think that the reason for my feet being unable to move was that one of the people lying in front of me had nailed my shoes to the floor.

My pastor friend and the preacher returned to the platform and closed the service with prayer with a vote of thanks to Almighty God for "saving this wonderful Jewish brother."

The pastor and the preacher sat down on the platform and as far as they were concerned, and as far as the congregation was concerned, the meeting apparently was over. For me it was just about to start.

I felt something or somebody take me bodily and move me towards the pulpit. I could never remember a time in my life that I was more terrified, but I had no resistance whatsoever. I stood in front of the pulpit trembling. The preacher noticed me standing there and walked towards the pulpit and looking over the top of it he asked, "What is it that you are wanting my dear Jewish brother?"

I looked at him and said, "Sir, somebody brought me here."

He looked from one side to the other and then said, "Brother, I don't see anybody."

I looked up at him again and said, "Sir, you might not see Him, but I can most surely feel Him."

He stood there looking down at me and I stood there looking up at him.

The next question that he asked me so lovingly and tenderly shocked me somewhat. "Do you want the Holy Ghost, dear brother?"

By this time I was trembling terribly. When he mentioned the word *Ghost* I kind of shied away from the pulpit. I did not like the word Ghost.

"Who gives that thing, sir?" I asked him, wondering what his reply would be.

He did not hesitate to answer me with one word, "Jesus."

"Sir," I said, "If Jesus gives that thing I want it, and I want it right now."

He smiled at me and said, "Brother Hymie, why don't you ask Him?"

I said, "Jesus, if you give people the Holy Ghost, will you kindly give it to me?" I intended continuing to ask Him for this Holy Ghost but found myself talking in a strange language which I did not understand. I had no control of my tongue that was bubbling out strange words in quick succession. My whole being felt so exalted, and I knew for the first time in my life that I was on *the main line* talking to my most wonderful Lord. I had the blessed assurance that He was not only listening to me but that I was getting through loud and clear, and that He was fully aware of what I was saying.

It must have been close to two hours that I stood there speaking this way, for when I ceased and turned to leave the whole congregation had left except my pastor friend, my new preacher friend and four other people standing in the foyer waiting for me. I felt so strong, so powerful, so God-conscious, and so in love with my new-found friend, Jesus.

67

Chapter Five
From Sinner to Stranger

The following morning I decided to get busy and win the world for Christ in a very short time.

The first one I planned to tell of my experience and lead to the Lord was my dear wife. As the disciple Andrew wanted to lead his brother Peter to the Master, so did I want to lead my wife to the Master. Andrew was more fortunate than I.

I rushed home to present my wife with a new husband. A husband God had cleansed, blessed, anointed and set free. A man who had now become perfect, holy and blessed in the sight of his Creator.

My pastor friend had given me a New Testament Bible as a gift. The first thing my wife noticed as I entered was the Bible under my arm and said, "Hymie, you should be ashamed of yourself."

I stood there surprised and could not understand why she had said this. Then she pointed to the Bible and said, "Why did you steal the Bible out of the hotel room?"

I looked at the Bible, looked at her, looked at the Bible again and said, "Honey, let me tell you what has happened to me. I have become a Christian. I have accepted Jesus Christ as my personal Lord and Saviour. He is my Master, my Messiah, and my ever reigning King. Honey, He has loosed me and I am free from sin, iniquity and worldliness. I have quit drinking and smoking and cursing and living a wild, reckless hellbound life. He has washed me in His precious blood, this lovely Jesus, and Honey, I stand here a new man, a changed man, and a Christian!"

I was most excited about this wonderful news that I could bring my wife, and waved my arms and jumped, much to her disgust.

She stood there shaking her head unable to comprehend what had happened to me. She shouted, "Go to bed, you're drunk again!"

I stood there thunderstruck by these words as she turned abruptly and walked into the bedroom, slamming the door. I recalled my pastor friend telling me that there would be many who would not understand what had taken place in my life. Now I could see that the very first one I had approached with this good news did not understand. I also recalled my pastor reading a verse of Scripture that had said Peter on the day of Pentecost and the others in the upper room also were accused of being drunk. Peter had replied, "These men are not drunk as you suppose."

I felt most unwanted in my own home.

It did not take my wife long to influence my three daughters and tell them that their father had become insane. They were afraid of me when I sat down at the same table. They were afraid to pass me in the hallway in case they might rub up against me, or touch me. My whole family did their best to avoid me in the house. What made it most difficult was the fact that now I loved my wife and my three girls more than I ever had before. I had such a desire now to hug them and love them and tell them how much I appreciated each one of them, but this was not to be.

Day after day I could feel the gap between my family and myself widen. Unbeknown to me, my wife had become a secret agent. She was going from one friend to the other with a petition to be signed by them. The petition stated that the undersigned were of the opinion that Mr. Hymie Rubenstein should be placed in a mental institution as soon as possible, as he had taken leave of his senses and was mad. I accidentally came across this petition, and after reading it I crossed out the word *mad* and substituted the word *glad.*

My wife and I were running a furniture store in Bloemfontein, in the Orange Free State, a province of South Africa. I would occasionally go into the store and my wife would avoid me. She would pay no attention to me whatsoever, even if I would speak to her and make some suggestion that I thought would benefit the business. There would be times I would burst into tears and weep under the anointing of the Holy Ghost, and that had the tendency to make her more afraid than ever.

One morning as my wife and I were working together in the office on some outstanding accounts, the telephone began ringing. I heard the ringing and looked at the telephone, but I seemed to forget that when a telephone rings one is supposed to lift the receiver and answer the call.

My wife sat there watching me, and I sat there watching the telephone. "Why on earth don't you answer that?" she yelled at me, and viciously grabbed for the receiver.

After answering the call and replacing the receiver she pleaded with me in a not-too-friendly manner to kindly please her and "get out of this office and never come back."

I began weeping, and with tears streaming down my face was leaving the building when my wife rushed to the office door and screamed, "I used to know you when you were a man but now you are even less than a mouse."

What puzzled me mostly was that my Jewish friends had now labeled me *mushumed* (madman). My Gentile friends had now labeled me "Crackpot."

As I walked downtown wondering why nobody seemed to be happy because I was happy, I noticed an elderly gentleman standing at the entrance of the Post Office. I walked up to him and spoke to him about the weather, and noticed that his hands and fingers and arms were badly misshapen. He saw me looking at these misshapen parts of his body, and immediately began to tell me how he had been suffering severely from crippling arthritis.

"I have been to the finest doctors in the city, and I have spent much money on practically every doctor that you can find listed in the book. For years I have been unable to receive any help whatsoever, and even medication does not help me anymore," he said sadly.

"I have a book that you might not have looked through," I told him. I noticed his curiosity. I pulled out the little book in my jacket pocket and showed him the title on the cover. He looked at it and said loudly, "Holy Bible."

I said, "Sir, there is one great physician in this book that you have failed to look into that will heal you without a prescription, without surgery, and without an appointment. Maybe you have overlooked this great physician, and I would highly recommend Him to you right now. His name is the

Lord Jesus Christ of Nazareth." I was so thrilled and happy that I would now be able to introduce this man to the other Man who could bring him constant relief.

I replaced my little black book into my pocket and was about to proceed to pray for him, but was startled to see the man jump away from me like a jack-in-the-box and run, as it were, for his life to take him away from this man who had spoken to him about a "Divine Healer."

Again I was puzzled. All I wanted to do was make unhappy people happy, make sad people glad, and make sick people well, by introducing them to my new found friend, Jesus.

This did not in any way discourage me. I noticed the cenotaph standing right near the center of the city square. My heart said to me, "Hymie, this is the ideal place to tell the heavy traffic about your wonderful friend, the Lord Christ Jesus." So I obeyed my heart and stood on the ready-made concrete platform at the cenotaph. In less than five minutes I had a fairly good congregation standing around listening to me tell them about the wonderful things that had taken place in my life, and just how wonderful it really was to be redeemed by the blood of the Lamb.

After twenty minutes there was scarcely standing room and I could see the hunger, the need, and the desire of the people to receive what I had received.

I myself was surprised at the power that was in my voice. It carried as well as any public address system could. I also noticed that many of my previous Jewish companions and their wives and children had also arrived on the scene. I learned later that they were keeping a check on my every movement, and would phone each other and make a report. I decided that I had certainly got the message across in my first "open-air meeting." I ended with a prayer of thanks to God, to his Son Jesus, and to the Holy Ghost. That service lasted approximately three hours.

As I started walking home I kept praising and thanking God that He had counted me faithful, allowing me to help the helpless. When I arrived home, the front door, which was usually left wide open, was locked. I put my ear to the door, and could hear the servant busy cooking in the kitchen. I walked around to the back of the house, and the servant spotted me through the window. As I reached to open the back door I heard it lock.

Strangely enough I was not annoyed. In the past I would more than likely have smashed the doors in. But now I seemed so calm, happy, and satisfied with everything and everybody. I sat down in the yard next to the pigeon hock I had built. Now and again I spotted one of my little girls peering out of the windows at me. Sometimes from their bedroom, sometimes from the kitchen window, and sometimes from the living room window. When I would wave happily to them they would scream with delight and run and report to Mama.

Eventually, when it was time to eat I heard the lock unlock. I walked into the kitchen and before I could greet anybody or say anything my wife let me know that she had already received reports from friends about "the spectacle you have made of yourself at the cenotaph today."

We all sat down to eat. I demanded that nobody put one morsel of food in their mouth until I said "Grace." Apart from the noise of the pots and the pans, the plates and the silver, not a word was spoken.

There was a knock at the front door. I went to answer and a neighbor was standing there very pale in his face.

"Can I help you, Mr. Smith?" I asked.

He proceeded to tell me that his eldest daughter was lying grievously sick, and that he would appreciate it very much if I would come and pray for her. I went to tell my wife that I wished to be excused. She sat there with wide-open eyes hardly believing that our neighbor had come to ask me, her husband, to come and pray.

I went into the sick girl's room and learned that the Smith family were Christians. We sat talking a while and then I laid my hands on the girl, as I had laid my hands on many at the cenotaph. She instantly fell asleep and the rest of the family and myself sat in the living room talking about the "wonderful power in the precious blood of the Lamb." This lasted until midnight and I returned home to find everybody had retired.

Early the following morning I walked into the kitchen

72

and found my wife most annoyed. It was not the first time that I had found her annoyed, but wondered why so early in the morning?

"Your kids are getting just as mad as you," she screamed at me.

I looked at her inquiringly.

"I found Leilah in the garage this morning choking the life out of our cat and screaming, "Come out of her, you dirty devil.""

Leilah had followed me down to the Smith home and watched me through the window praying for the young Smith girl.

I did not see that anybody intended making any breakfast so I left for the office. When I arrived there, there were quite a few people standing in the doorway. This pleased me because I thought that they were customers who were waiting to buy furniture. I also thought that if I could have a few good sales I would be able to phone my wife and tell her about it. That I knew would make her happy, and I surely wanted to get rid of that misery she had adopted of late.

To my surprise the people had come for prayer. They had heard about my first open-air service at the cenotaph, and quite a few testified that they had received instantaneous healings. Others had testified to the fact that they had been healed on their way home after prayer. The word had got around that there was a "faith healer" in the city.

The truck driver was there and I told him that I had left my keys in the office, so he looked at me very suspiciously and unlocked the door. Apparently he had also been injected with fear by my wife.

I sat with the people in the store, on the furniture, and counseled with them. After counselling I decided that it was time for me to pray for them individually. I became a bit concerned about the fact that I might be distracted while praying for them by customers walking in and out so I locked the main entrance.

One by one I took my patients into my private office and prayed for them. The only thing that mattered to me was that they would know and feel the beautiful Holy Spirit of God, and know and meet the real person, Jesus.

How long it was that I prayed and counseled with these people I do not know, but as I unlocked the door and bid them farewell, I was shocked to see Mrs. Rubenstein standing there, along with other customers. Some of them were our best buyers from the biggest furniture and department stores in the city. Most of them were Jewish.

My enraged wife angrily pushed past me shouting, "How on earth do you ever expect to do business with the doors closed? How on earth do you ever expect to make a living by locking the buyers out?"

It was obvious that our customers had also been informed about my strange antics, and I noticed that there was a tendency for them to hide behind the furniture. I decided that it would be wise to leave.

A few nights later as I was shaving and preparing to go to the weekly Wednesday evening prayer meeting, I noticed Leilah, our eldest girl, standing in the bathroom doorway. I asked her how she was, and was afraid to reach for her thinking that she would run away screaming for her mama. But she looked at me with those beautiful baby-blue eyes and said, "Daddy, can I please come to the church with you."

I was more than overjoyed by her request, and also very much surprised. I asked her whether she had mentioned this to her mother, and she assured me that her mama had told her that if her father was prepared to take her that she could go along "at your own risk." That night it was my joy and pleasure to take my daughter to a Christian church.

No sooner had we returned home than Leilah ran to her mama to tell her what had taken place in the church. Leilah seemed pleased and excited about her new experience, and I walked into the room to hear what she had to say.

"Well, dear," my wife asked her, "How did you enjoy your first introduction to the church where they talk about Jesus?"

My daughter replied that she had thoroughly enjoyed it "to a point."

Both my wife and I looked at her inquiringly.

"What do you mean, dear?" my wife asked.

Leilah looked at me as though she was afraid to speak any further. My wife recognized the look of fear on her face

74

and said, "What on earth has your mad dad done this time?"

The girl seemed to be reluctant to answer. Then she said, "Well, Ma, while everybody else was standing in prayer with their hands in the air and their eyes tightly shut, Daddy was rolling under the seats."

My wife jumped to her feet screaming and shouting, cursing and swearing. Nothing seemed to be right that I was doing, but I was thoroughly enjoying it.

The visits by the sick to the store continued and the locking of the door continued also. One afternoon after lunch quite a few members of the Salvation Army paid me a visit. They asked me whether I would give them my testimony.

As we sat inside the store I began to tell them of my born-again experience. To avoid any distraction I had once again locked the door. This had become customary, much to the annoyance of my customers, my buyers, and above all, my wife. The Salvation Army people congratulated me on the fine work I had been doing at the cenotaph, Post Office, and also my new preaching place outside the Cinema.

That evening when I arrived home the welcome was worse than ever. My wife suggested that we either sell the business, or that I quit the madness. "It is utterly impossible for us to make a living the way that you are carrying on," she shouted. She said that that month the door was closed more than it was open, and again asked me how any business could thrive with a locked door.

I promised her that if that particular month's business was worse than any month in the past four and a half years, I would immediately cease to do the things that I was doing with regard to my new Christian life. She looked at me unbelievingly. I promised her never to pray again, never to preach again, never to testify again, and above all never to lock the door again.

At the end of that month my wife gathered all the sales books, checkbooks and whatever other books she could grab ahold of and locked herself away in her office with what I called the "Jewish piano." Others call it the National Cash Register.

I could hear her ringing and ringing that machine.

After some time she came out of the office. I did not know how business could possibly be done the way that I was trying to do it. Humanly speaking, it was impossible to sell and earn money when the people who were supposed to buy and supply the money were hindered from doing so.

My wife looked puzzled, and I said, "Well, dear, was this month's business worse than any month in the four and a half years that we have been here?"

She replied indirectly by saying, "How do you expect to do business with the doors locked?"

I said, "Will you please answer my question?"

And then she said, "Why do you not allow our customers to smoke in the store?" I could see she was now trying to avoid my question.

"Honey, I am asking you once again to please tell me if this month's business was worse than any month in the four and a half years that we have been here?"

Again she did not reply to my question, but said, "Why do you go around sticking labels with Christian texts all over the furniture?"

I now became impatient because I wanted a truthful answer from her. I just stood looking at her defying her to give me a negative answer. She slammed down the bundle of books she was carrying on to an arm chair nearby and marched out of the store shouting, "I can't understand how anyone can do business with doors locked!" That was the best month in four and a half years!

I locked the door and fell on my knees and looked up and told Almighty God how much I appreciated Him for never failing me. I believe that that was one of the greatest signs that my wife had ever witnessed.

The following Sunday she told me she would like to accompany me to the church. I was afraid to show how thrilled I was by her request in case I might cause her to change her mind.

We drove up alongside the church and found that there were many cars and much people. The service had just begun and my wife motioned to me that she would like to go to the ladies room. I waited in the foyer and was surprised to see her come out again immediately in a fit of temper. Before I could ask her what had upset her, she marched out of the building into the car. I climbed into the car next to her as she kept saying, "Pigs, pigs, nothing but dirty pigs."

I did not know what to say and thought for the moment that once again she had found an excuse to find fault with me and other believers. She explained that somebody had been in the toilet before her and had not flushed the tank. Being a spotlessly clean family, I myself was most disappointed that this should have happened, and also felt that it was nothing but a trick of Satan to keep my wife out of the church.

My apologies did not help, but the following morning Willie Smit, the pastor, paid us a visit. He was very pleasant, and I liked him exceptionally well. My wife probably at that time had other ideas about him, but when he started to use the office telephone at random without asking permission first, this gave her new ammunition to bombard both me and the other Christians.

Instead of things improving, they gradually became worse.

After we had written out our own personal salary check I informed my wife that it was necessary to make out another check to the church. "What has our salary got to do with the church?" she asked, placing the checkbook back in her purse.

I motioned to her to extract the checkbook out of the purse and write a check equivalent to the tenth of what we had earned, explaining to her that this was known as tithing. I did my best to explain the tithe, and she did her best to persuade me otherwise. On this matter I decided to be forceful for the first time.

As she once again opened her handbag to get out her compact, I pulled away the handbag with my left hand and grabbed the checkbook with my right hand and slammed it down on the table, demanding that she write the check for the tithes, or else I would be forced to write it myself. She was more than surprised to see the stand that I was now making, and wrote out the tithing check.

As I moved around from town to town selling my wares business became more prosperous than we could have hoped for. The news had spread about me among the travelers, the buyers, and the stores. I found that many of the buyers whom I had notified about my calling on them on certain dates would be waiting for me in the doorway of their stores to hand me the orders. This they did to prevent me going inside of the store, and getting rid of me as soon as possible.

I arrived at a town called Clocolan. On the market square stood a cenotaph. To me a cenotaph meant only one thing—a ready-made pulpit. I was not interested now in selling furniture in the town, my first duty was to tell about the grace of God. This I did waving my Bible high in the air, and telling those who were gathering all about "the way, the truth, and the life." I extended an invitation but there was no response. This was discouraging, but I felt that my mission had been somehow, someway accomplished.

I crossed over the road and a man standing in a shoe store motioned to me with both arms. I could see that he was really excited about something and walked up to him to see the cause for the excitement.

He looked at me, grabbed my arm and began weeping. "Five minutes before you arrived young man, I had decided to drive to the river and shoot myself," he said. He took a gun out of his pocket and showed it to me. "As I walked toward my car to do this thing, I heard you shouting from the cenotaph. I stood right here and listened to what you had to say about the Prince of Peace, about the way He stopped you from doing the very thing that I was just about to do. As you spoke I allowed that same Jesus to do for me what He has done for you!"

I walked away from the man rejoicing, knowing that a new name had been written down in Glory.

The first furniture store I walked into after that some-one was waiting for me. Not in the doorway this time, but sitting in the office writing out a full-sized order for me. The owner of the store explained how he had called his whole staff to the sidewalk to listen to my message of deliverance, love, faith and power. He told me that he was an elder in his church, and that there should be more such as I, bringing the good news to God's people.

I left him with the blessed assurance that I would not only return but that I would make it my business to use the pulpit which I felt had been supplied me, right in the middle of the city.

That night after supper I went directly to my room. No longer did I need the pool table for entertainment, or the smoking room for relaxation, or the bar for company as I had now found all the entertainment that I needed in the wonderful and thrilling Word of Almighty God. I loved to read the Bible and learn about the way God guided, blessed, saved and sanctified. It thrilled me to no extent.

Some of my business in the furniture line had to be done in the town of Bethlehem in South Africa. I was compelled to spend the weekend in that city as it was 350 miles away from my home. My procedure was to work my way back home from town to town and from village to village.

On Sunday morning I walked into a church and the pastor welcomed me. When I mentioned my name I was surprised to learn that he had already heard about me. "We would be thrilled if you would give us your testimony here this morning," he suggested.

After the service the pastor invited those who wished to, to remain and go to the back of the platform into the prayer room to pray. I joined the group of perhaps 60 in the prayer room. We all knelt to glorify the name of Jesus. I felt impressed (as some prayed, some wept, and others prayed in tongues) that God wanted to show that He appreciated our prayers.

I did not know how, why, or when, but suddenly one of the side doors of the prayer room opened and I noticed a lady leading a young man. I saw that the young man was blind. Somehow I knew that this was the gift of miracles that God was going to give to the group that kneeled there praying.

I stood to my feet and asked for the attention of the group as the mother and her blind son stood there. I told the group that I felt very strongly that God wanted them to witness that He was God and not a man that He should lie. Without any further hesitation I laid my hands on the boy and prayed a simple prayer, asking the same Jesus who had opened blind eyes before, to open the blind eyes of this young man. Again without hesitation I turned about and walked to the other side of the long room, and took a half crown out of my pocket (which is a fairly large silver coin), holding it high in the air and asked the young man, "What do you see?" He was weeping and could not answer. But by the screams and the yells of the prayer warriors that stood nearby I knew that that same eye-opening Jesus had once again performed a miracle.

Like lightning this news spread around the city. The church board asked me if I could possibly hold a revival. I hated to decline, but felt in all fairness to my wife I should work my way back home. Nevertheless, I agreed to speak again that night. Needless to say the church was fully packed, and there was scarcely standing room on the outside.

I worked my way back to my hometown and found business all along the way to be great. I knew that I had an understanding with my heavenly Father: "If I would work with Him, He would work for me."

The following Sunday morning I asked my wife if she would please come to church with me. She seemed to be less hostile towards me over the past few weeks, and she accepted my invitation.

As we walked into the church I prayed that she would not look for the ladies room again. God answered my prayer, and we took our seats in a very crowded church. The 75-member choir filled the air with such wonderful spirit of love. The waving of many handkerchiefs in praise were seen in use, including my own.

After the choir had been seated I raised my hands and began to speak loudly in an unknown tongue. Somebody close by brought the interpretation, and the congregation unanimously praised the Lord. I sat down and my wife leaned over to me and said, "Hymie, I did not know that you spoke Yiddish so fluently." I gave no answer as I knew it would only confuse her.

Pastor Willie Smit walked behind the pulpit with a newspaper in his hand. He explained that it was not a habit of his to ever read the newspaper, and that this was the first time in his long ministry that he had brought a worldly newspaper into his church. But he opened the paper and read how a young converted Jewish traveler had stayed in Bethlehem for the weekend and visited a church there. Then read the full account of what had transpired there—how God had heard the prayer of this traveler and opened the eyes of a young boy who had been totally blind for the past fourteen years. When he concluded he asked the congregation to rise and thank Jesus that He was the same yesterday, today and forever.

After much praise the congregation was seated and the pastor said, "Friends, that young converted Jewish traveler is in this congregation, and I want him to come up to the platform." This was most unexpected, especially for the lady who sat next to me.

While I took the opportunity to lift up the name of Jesus a man jumped up a short way from the platform in the center of his row. I noticed him beckoning to me with both hands. Although I could see that he was shouting at me, I became totally deaf. The man then sat down and I was sure that he had been complimenting me about the way God had used me in Bethlehem.

It did not take me long to find out that I was totally incorrect. As I was driving home my wife moved closer to me and held me lightly by the arm. (This action was worth more than all the tea in China, and all the gold in South Africa.) "Hymie," she said softly, "I can see that God has really done a work in your life. I now understand what you mean when you say that you have been born again and that God has saved you and changed you."

I remained silent as we continued our journey home.

"Hymie, can I ask you something?"

"What is it, honey?" I asked.

"Did you hear what that man said to you and called you while you stood behind the pulpit? That man who jumped up in front of you and waved his fists at you, did you hear him?"

"No," I replied. "As a matter of fact, my ears seemed to have been close the moment he jumped up."

"Just as well, I guess," she said.

"Why?" I asked, very much surprised.

She told me that that man had stood there denouncing

me as one of the false prophets that Jesus had spoken about. He had also commanded me to "Shut your big Jewish mouth, or I will come up there and shut it for you."

Chapter Six
Working in the Vineyard

It was very difficult for me to believe that a so-called Christian would publicly insult me in the house of God. Also in the presence of such a large gathering. Strangely enough, I was surprised at the amount of compassion and forgiveness I had for him.

I told my wife I felt no animosity whatsoever, and reminded her that if that would have taken place a short time ago that same man who insulted me would have been a hopeless hospital case. She fully agreed and said that it amazed her that I was not annoyed.

Sometime later I was invited one weekend to speak once again in the church in Bethlehem. I accepted the invitation.

Early that Sunday morning there was a knock on my hotel room door and a young boy stood outside with a magazine in his hand. He opened the magazine and asked me to read the article in it. He left and I relaxed in bed reading an article which denounced all religions that believed that God was a reality.

I was amazed to read how some of the world's finest preachers were brought down. How some of the leading university professors, lecturers and teachers had proved or tried to prove, that Almighty God was not a reality. There were other articles from parents who had forbidden their children to ever read the Bible. Some went so far as to say they would rather hang their children before they would allow them to get involved with Christianity.

I began to weep as I considered the blindness of all these people. I fell to my knees and apologized to the Father and the Son and the Holy Ghost on behalf of all those people who had written those articles. I had never heard of visions before, but as I kneeled there suddenly I saw Jesus hanging from a cross. I was viewing Him from the side and his long, black curly matted hair hung in front of his face as his head hung low and his arms and feet were nailed to the cross. I began to weep and could not control the weeping.

That morning in the church I explained to the pastor what I had seen, and as I spoke to the people I could not control my weeping. So much so that before the service closed there was not a dry eye in the congregation.

I returned to my room, and once more fell on my knees asking God to forgive.

I felt impressed to go to the city of Johannesburg and challenge the editor of the magazine that I had read that morning.

The following day instead of heading back for home I decided to head for Johannesburg as an ambassador of the Lord Jesus Christ. As I traveled through the country I passed many farm lands. On the one particular farm I noticed a flock of sheep running wildly hither and thither. I could see that something was wrong, and at first thought that a snake was probably terrorizing them. I stopped when I noticed the carcass of a young lamb fall out of the sky. There were six large vultures terrorizing the flock and viciously grabbing hold of the baby lambs, carrying them high into the sky and tearing them apart. I felt heartsore as I watched the sheep try to protect their lambs, but they had no means of defense.

I began to honk my horn hoping that would frighten off the vultures, but it didn't. I climbed out of the car and screamed loudly at them, but that had no effect. I looked around for the shepherd, but there was no shepherd there.

I hastily jumped into my car and drove to the nearest farm house. Mr. Jannie DuPlessis met me, as I climbed out of the car. I explained what was happening down on the nearby farm. He and six others climbed in a truck with their rifles hoping to destroy the vultures. I followed in my car.

When we arrived the vultures had already left. Mr. DuPlessis and the men climbed over the fence and collected fourteen carcasses. He returned and explained that the owner of the sheep had gone on vacation, and that it was more than likely that the shepherd was lying somewhere probably drunk and fast asleep.

He invited me to his home for lunch. He had a large

family, and we gathered around the family table and enjoyed a wonderful lunch of roast lamb and hot vegetables.

"Mr. Rubenstein, can you please explain why you were so concerned about somebody else's sheep being destroyed by those vultures?" Jannie asked.

The little that I had learned about the psalmist David and his twenty-third psalm came to my mind. I told him how God was concerned about His sheep and because of that I was concerned.

"Mr. Rubenstein, I understand from your name that you are a Jewish man. Yet you talk so lovingly and freely about your wonderful Messiah Jesus. How is it that you as a Jewish man believe in Jesus of Nazareth?"

This was a wonderful opportunity for me to take off and tell the story of my conversion. I practically exploded as I told them about the sea-walker, the blind-man healer, and the light of the world. My testimony left them dumbfounded.

As we sat there meditating on what we had heard I looked out of the window and noticed that there were large groups of laborers sitting around idle. There were many tractors and other harvesting implements and large machines also standing around. I looked at Mr. DuPlessis and said, "Sir, why is it that these people sit around and all this machinery stands idle—nobody is working?"

He looked at his wife and then at his mother and then at the children and began telling me about the worst experience the farmers had had in many years. How the lice plague had spread across the land and had eaten every stalk of wheat that had grown. He pointed out of the window and said, "As far as your eyes can see that used to be wheat fields, but now they look like stretches of desert."

A hush had fallen over the family, and I could tell this tragedy had deeply affected everyone.

He further explained how this horrible plague had brought about unemployment and had also caused a great shortage of many things. "Even the banks have been so badly affected that they are considering closing." I was sure he wiped tears from his eyes.

I sat there sympathizing with him for a while. Then felt impressed to say, "Sir, why don't you trust God to move the lice out of your wheat fields? Why don't you walk into those fields and command the lice to leave immediately in the name of Jesus?"

The family just looked at one another in amazement. They then all stared at me as though I had taken leave of my senses. I said no more, for I felt I had said all I had to say.

There was a long silence and then Mrs. DuPlessis said to me, "If you believe that way, and if you have that faith, why don't you go down and command the lice to leave our wheat fields?"

I looked at the farmer and waited to see his reaction.

"Do you really think He could do such a thing?" he asked me.

"He did it for Moses, Sir, and I am fully persuaded that if He removed the lice when Moses asked him to, He will remove the lice when I ask Him to."

Again there was a long silence.

"Would you go down and remove them then?" he asked.

I obliged by walking through the fields commanding the lice to leave in the name of Jesus. Then drove back to my hotel room.

The following morning I drove out to see Mr. Jannie DuPlessis. I could see that his wife had become afraid of me. I asked where her husband was and she ran into the house without replying, but I could hear her shouting at the top of her voice, "Here's that man, here's that man, here's that man."

I walked inside the house uninvited and sat down in the living room. The farmer walked in very slowly nodding his head from side to side. It was not necessary for me to ask him what had happened, but it was the only correct thing to do.

He explained that he had gone through forty acres of land and could find no lice.

I asked the family to stand in reverence as I prayed and thanked God that He was still the lice-removing God.

I now left for Johannesburg to challenge the people who had written the articles in that magazine. I was more loaded with heavenly power than ever.

Upon my arrival in the city I went to the publishing

company. I walked in with my large black book under my arm and went into the office marked: Secretary. I explained that I wished to see the editor of the magazine. I laid the magazine in front of her. She looked at the black book under my arm and excused herself.

She came back and said the publisher was not there. I knew she was not telling the truth. I then asked to see the author of that particular story and told her to be sure that she found him and not return with another untruth.

A short while later she arrived with five men who asked me to accompany them.

We walked up a flight of stairs into a large office. There was a large Imbuia table in the center with very attractive chairs around it. We all sat down. The man who sat at the head of the table introduced himself as the manager of the firm and asked me what my business was.

I explained who I was, and why I was there. The group seemed to be much relieved. One of the men gave a sigh of relief as he said, "When we saw that big black book that you are carrying, we thought that you were a counselor coming to lay a charge against us."

Everyone laughed except I. "Gentlemen, let me tell you that the counselor is right here in our midst," I said. They looked at one another, but I continued. I told them that I had come to challenge the editor of the magazine, the author of the story, the professors, the teachers, and the students who were responsible for this story to be printed in their magazine.

There was a deep silence in the room for a long time. Then the editor looked at me with a sneer on his face and said, "What proof have you that there is a God, and that He is alive?"

I did not fail to tell them of many healings I had seen. I also told of many letters that I could produce testifying to the power of a real live God.

I noticed two or three of them nudge one another, and heard such words as, "crackpot, weirdo, fanatic, psycho," etc. One of them turned to me angrily and said, "We are a busy publishing company, and we know your type."

"What do you mean by that uncalled-for remark?" I

asked, making sure that they would in no way discard me.

He explained that so many people were looking for publicity, and trying to make headline news that they were "sick and tired of the whole business."

I looked directly at the man who sat at the head of the table and with all the authority that I knew was at my disposal said, "Sir, in the name of the Lord Christ Jesus I challenge you and these other gentlemen who are present, and your staff and every member of the university that was instrumental in this story to meet me at any place of their choosing and I will prove to you and all these others that the God of Abraham and Isaac and Jacob is very much alive these days."

"The proof that you talk about is not sufficient, and does not warrant us to do what you have requested us to do," one of them stated.

The story of Mr. DuPlessis flashed into my mind and without hesitation told them the story. They feasted on every word. I related that this farmer was skeptical, an unbeliever as they were, an elder in the same church organization as they belonged to, but was no longer skeptical.

The director said he would make further inquiries during the day and if I would come early the following morning he would arrange for both a newsman and photographer to accompany me to that farm.

I left there satisfied that I had fully accomplished what I had been impressed to do.

That evening I stayed in my dad's hotel, and early the next morning before daybreak I was waiting outside the publishing building. To my surprise I did not have to wait long. It appeared the news reporter and the cameraman were waiting for me. I knew that God had everything under control.

I greeted the men jovially, but the response was not encouraging at all.

The news reporter motioned to a car, letting me know that we would go in that car. I noticed it was a brand new Chevrolet, and very attractive. I climbed into the back seat while the two men got into the front.

I said, "Gentlemen, I thank you for assisting me in putting out this challenge, but I want you to know right at the commencement of this business that the enemy Lucifer will do all that he possibly can to prevent us from doing this work." It was as though I had been speaking to the windshield.

They appeared to simply ignore me, until the news reporter placed the key in the ignition and turned the switch. The three of us were shocked when there was a sudden explosion under the hood of the car. They jumped out quickly, opened the hood as clouds of smoke filled the air.

I climbed out and stood next to them. They looked around for another means of transportation, and the photographer pointed to his small car that stood nearby and said, "I think it will be a good idea to use my car."

His friend did not seem to approve of the suggestion, and seemed to be bent on cancelling the whole thing.

I held him by the arm and said with much authority, "Sir, you have been delegated to do a job, and you had better see that you do it, and that you do it well." The man who was already afraid of me now became terrified. I don't know whether it was my six-foot-two height, or the 210 pounds that frightened him, or the authority that had been given to me, but like a little dog with his tail between his legs he climbed into the small car and slammed the door viciously.

I climbed in on the other side and sat in the back as the photographer started his car wondering if it, too, would perhaps explode.

As we travelled along the road they spoke very little apart from a few remarks about the hills, animals and scenery. I asked if they would mind if I told my life story. There was no response whatsoever, so I began.

We were travelling up a rather steep incline and the engine began to misfire. They instantly looked at one another wondering whether this was to be the second explosion. The engine sputtered, the car shuddered and we were jerked to and fro.

"Pull off the side of the road," I commanded. The driver pulled off the road and brought the car to a halt. I repeated what I had told them at the outset. Then I said, "Gentlemen, if you will kindly close your eyes and bow your heads and place a bit of faith and trust in God I will pray a prayer of faith and in the name of Jesus cast out of that engine the thing that is trying to hinder our progress."

I could see that they were confused and unaware of what I was about to do. They just sat there like a pair of mummies looking directly to the front. I leaned forward and pushed their heads down and began to pray. It was a short prayer but big enough to accomplish what it had intended to accomplish. "We can carry on now, the job has been done," I told them.

We took off once again on our journey with no trouble whatsoever. As we passed through a city the driver looked in his rear view mirror and said very apologetically, "Sir, do you mind very much if I would pull into the nearest service station and just ask a mechanic there to check my engine?"

I told him if that was what he wanted to do he was free to do what he wanted to.

We drove into a station into the workshop. We all climbed out and I was glad to stretch my long legs which had been uncomfortably tucked under me in the back of the small car. The mechanic was told what had happened along the road as he lifted the hood of the car and began examining the engine.

He then removed the four spark plugs and gasped in amazement. He cursed and said that it was impossible for any engine to function with such spark plugs. They were totally burned away except for the white top. Then he said, "Gentlemen, only a prayer could have brought you this far." My two associates looked at each other but not at me.

I walked out of that garage with my hands in the air thanking God once again that He was God.

I noticed a block away from the garage a Post Office. A Post Office and a cenotaph spelled one word: pulpit. I walked to the Post Office and stood behind the red mailbox on the sidewalk and once again advertised the Prince of Peace, Jesus the Lord, and the Holy Ghost the Comforter.

A short while later I noticed the car coming out of the service station and pulling up nearby to the red mailbox, and my two friends sat there listening with the others that had gathered around. I realized that there was unfortunately no time to make an altar call as I was busy in another "witnessing department."

I climbed back into the car and we continued on our

journey. We arrived at our destination in the darkness. We were invited in and because the men were from Mr. DuPlessis' denomination he was willing to keep them overnight.

Mr. DuPlessis, and the rest of his family, confirmed the story I had told them earlier in the publishing house. We went in the morning to the land that was once infested with lice. I could not only see little tusks of wheat growing, but I could also feel that Somebody holy and blessed had most certainly been on that land.

The photographer instructed the farmer and myself where to stand, and as I held my large black book in my hand opened to Psalm 23 the farmer looked down into the Bible. It was as though a blanket of peace and love and joy was thrown over the four of us. The photographer could not take the photo as he was weeping. The reporter could not write his report as he was weeping. The farmer and myself stood there and made up a foursome of weeping men.

After a while we slightly recovered and photos were taken. The men from the publishing company thanked the farmer for his assistance, as well as the wonderful night they had so enjoyed. I thanked the farmer for his assistance and we left for Johannesburg.

My two friends had now become very conversant and friendly, bombarding me with questions about my past, my present, and my future. The miles and the time quickly slipped away. As they came to a halt and bade me farewell it was with a sore heart that I had to leave them. I could see that they felt the same way about my departure.

The following edition of the magazine thrilled me beyond my wildest dreams. There were full pages of photos taken down on the farm. The article written by the news reporter I could feel was promulgated by the Holy Ghost. The article concluded with the challenge that I had submitted to those who so easily denied a living God. The reporter concluded by asking those who doubted and denied belief in a living God to explain the wonderful miracle that had happened on the Jannie DuPlessis farm.

Thousands of letters arrived from all around the country. Some congratulating me on the strong stand I had taken. Others asked for prayer. The needs of the multitudes were brought to my attention, and I longed to feed the hearts of so many that hungered and thirsted after righteousness.

I sent a copy of the magazine to David DuPlessis, a South African theologian in the United States of America and asked him to translate the news story from the South African into English. He obliged and had it not only translated but inserted in one of the leading American Christian magazines. The response from this was enormous, and proved that through this story the faith of thousands of God's children had been lifted high.

I was now totally and fully committed to God. I had forgotten about my business responsibilities, knowing full well that I was now about "my Father's business" which was the most important of all businesses.

I thought much about my wife and my three lovely daughters, but knew that the time would come when they would appreciate the stand that I had now made.

I went to a boarding house in one of the suburbs of Johannesburg and decided to "get away and come apart with God." I explained to the two ladies who assured me that they were Christians, what my intentions were. "I want you to lock me up in my room for three days," I told them, "from Wednesday night sunset to Friday night sunset, and then unlock the door."

Although they understood what I had asked them to do, they still appeared to be nervous and wished to make one or two suggestions about drinking water and a periodic snack. I said I appreciated their suggestions but would only stay if things were carried out according to my plans.

They agreed, so for three days I called upon the Lord.

For three days He blessed me and not a morsel of food or a drop of water passed my lips. The third evening as I looked out of the window watching the sun setting in the west I could scarcely stand. All strength had drained out of my body. My beard had grown. Yet I felt that I had received much of God.

The door was unlocked and it seemed as though the ladies were relieved to find I had not died. One stood there with a glass of orange juice and the other with buttered toast.

I noticed a young girl standing behind them. They

placed the juice and toast on a small table near my bed and then asked the young girl to come in. They explained that the girl had a cancer in her left breast. She burst out crying and said, "Please, Sir, help me."

I knew that with the power I had received during that fasting time that cancer would have to go. I told her so and placed my arm around her as we kneeled to ask the "remover of cancer" to remove hers.

During the evening I relaxed sipping glasses of water and orange juice.

Early the next morning one of the owners of the boarding house received a phone call. It was a call from the young girl I had prayed for that evening. In between her crying and her screaming she had told how she had awakened that morning to find that the small peach-like cancer had fallen out of her left breast.

If I could speak with the tongues of men and of angels I could never ever tell how much it meant to me as I recognized that once again I had become an instrument in the hands of the "Great Physician."

At that time there were two powerful church denominations that were holding large tent conventions in the city. I knew that I was free to go to either of them, and that I would be warmly received. Yet I felt in my heart that I wanted to be in the one that the good Lord would have me to be in. Like an answer to prayer a pastor arrived from one of the conventions, and invited me to accompany him to the city of Benoni. He introduced himself to me as Pastor LeRoux.

We arrived at the grounds where an extraordinarily large tent stood. It was a green tent with very many poles, and there were thousands of people inside as well as outside. The car parks were filled to capacity.

It was a Saturday night and the chairman announced the future meetings to a crowd of approximately 9,000 people. He asked if I would give my testimony Monday evening. He announced from the pulpit that a Jewish business man would be giving his testimony of how he came "out of darkness into God's wonderful light."

One of the members of the committee later explained

that it was a good idea for me to have been given the Monday night, as that was the quietest night of the week, and a smaller crowd would not frighten me. I appreciated his concern.

To the surprise of many the Monday night attendance overshadowed the Saturday and Sunday night attendances. I had made many notes which I had stuffed in my Bible, and intended using these to put more emphasis and power into my testimony.

As usual, before walking to the pulpit I was nervous. As usual, the palms of my hands had become wet. I entered in with everybody else singing the wonderful praises to a wonderful God. As I addressed the large congregation, I was astonished to find that as I spoke both the listeners and myself had no idea of what I was speaking about. A strange language poured out of my mouth and I became most embarrassed. I stopped for a while wondering what to do. I had not bargained for this, and I knew that all the notes I had made—none of them corresponded to this. I tried again to address the people, more loudly this time, trusting that this time everyone would understand what I was talking about. But it was no different.

I stood there contemplating my next move. I thought that it would be proper to step away from the pulpit in order to allow somebody else to take over. I thought, *third time lucky*. Again I shouted, this time even louder, but no change whatsoever. The strange language kept pouring out more quickly than before. I looked down to my left side and noticed a man sitting in the second row with a pair of crutches lying against the seat in front of him. Somehow there was an instant connection between that man and myself, and I knew that God had brought about this connection.

I pointed my finger at the crippled man and said with much boldness, "Sir, stand to your feet and be healed in the name of Jesus." I was happy that now I was speaking in a tongue that both the audience and myself understood.

The man struggled to his feet and held tightly to the seat in front of him. I prayed a prayer of faith and asked the man to let go of the chair, to raise his hands and thank his Healer, Jesus, the King of glory. He did not respond in any way but held tight the chair in front of him.

I was surprised at the response and called down to him very loudly, "How do you feel now after my prayer, my dear brother?"

It was a strange experience for me as the man hollered back as loudly as he possibly could, "I feel worse now than I felt when I walked into the tent. As a matter of fact, I feel worse now than I have ever felt in my life."

I did not know what to do in this case, and knew that all the notes that I had stuffed into the Bible were once again useless to me in this instance. I knew, that I knew, that I knew God intended both to try my patience, faith and perseverance.

"Come and stand here in this middle aisle," I said to the man.

The people in the row stood up as the man had much difficulty carrying both himself and his crutches into the middle aisle. He stood before me leaning on his crutches and looking up into my face as though to say, "Well, big shot, what are you going to try now?"

After a short pause I began with a demanding voice to speak in a strange tongue directly to the crippled man who stood before me. Suddenly like a rocket that man shot up into the air. The one crutch flew to the left side and one crutch flew to the right side and the man went walking, leaping, and shouting and crying and praising God.

As he ran by row after row the sick in each row were completely delivered and healed. The crippled man had run to the rear end of the tent and back to the pulpit where many others who were healed stood to welcome him, and if ever the great Christ of Nazareth received a rousing welcome, He received it that night!

I began to feel that if I really believed what I believed I believed, I should resign from business and go full time into "my Father's business."

One evening as I was lifting up the only begotten Son of God, a man walked into the tent carrying a little girl in his arms. He came and stood below me near the pulpit. As I continued speaking and not knowing exactly what to do about this unexpected interference, I examined the young girl he was holding. She had braces around her waist and down both legs.

Other pastors went to ask the man what he wanted, but he kept pointing at me showing that he just had to speak to me. I apologized to the audience for the disturbance and asked them just to be patient for a short while. I kneeled down on the platform and listened to what the man had to say.

"Brother Hymie, I do not know this little girl I am carrying, but she has been standing at the wire fence that runs alongside the camping grounds. She says that she looked down alongside the fence and saw a man all dressed in white walking toward her. Brother Hymie, she did not know who the man was but she was sure that she had seen pictures of him before in the Sunday school, and that the man looked very much like the man in the pictures of Jesus. She told me that He took her by the shoulders and turned her slowly around so that she was not only facing the tent but that she was looking directly at you. That man in the white robe then said to her, "Go to that man that you are looking at and he will heal you.""

As I explained to the audience what had taken place there was weeping, shouting, screaming, and praising God. Once again I did not know what procedure a man had to adopt in such a situation.

I bent down and lifted the body of that four-year-old blonde-headed girl. I held her tightly in my arms and looked up to the Great Creator of heaven and earth and asked Him to give to this beautiful young girl a perfect and sound body. I felt a certain amount of uncertainty but it did not remain too long.

I handed her to the man. As he placed her upon his knee and began talking to her and stroking her long blonde hair I said to him, "Get these iron braces off her, please, Sir, immediately."

I went on to talk to the congregation who were now excitedly waiting to see the miracle-working power of God in His Son Christ Jesus. Much praise and thanksgiving went up to God.

The iron leggings and braces had been removed and the

young girl was still sitting on the man's lap. I took her in my arms and as I walked back to the pulpit she wriggled out of my arms to the floor. She jumped from the floor onto a shelf that had been fitted behind the pulpit, and from there onto the top of the round half-circle pulpit itself. She did a kind of dance around the top of the pulpit, waving her hands frantically. Then she jumped from the top of the pulpit onto the platform and from the platform onto the floor below, and ran outside the tent screaming, "Mama, Mama, Mama, it is Jesus who has healed me."

There was no more doubt in my mind that I had no time left to *consider* going into the full-time ministry. God had proved himself, and I was more than willing to allow Him to continue proving himself through me.

I did not know what one was supposed to do when he took a stand on a full-time basis. After nineteen years in that boat, I am still trying to find out.

I made up my mind that, regardless of what any man might say, I would continue loving the Lord. I was determined to give water to the thirsty, healing to the sick, encouragement to the discouraged, gladness to the sad, joy to the troubled and love to the lost.

Pastor Peter Snyman invited me to a nearby city, Klerksdorp.

His congregation had erected a large-sized green tent that stood practically in the center of the city. Klerksdorp was one of the richest gold-mining areas in the world. Extremely wealthy.

It was strange that the man David Bairus, who had turned "king's evidence" in my court case back in Kimberly, lived there. Only a short time before this I had driven around Klerksdorp hoping to find this man. It was through his witness that I had lost everything. I carried a revolver with me then, and was determined to both find him and kill him. During my inquiries I had been told that David Bairus rode a bicycle to work each morning. I had contemplated riding over him, and destroying him either that way or the gun.

Now I sat in my car meditating. I was both nervous and excited about the tent services. I took a quick gasp of breath; walking across the intersection was the very man I had wanted to destroy. David Bairus was just about to walk by my car when I turned down the window and shouted, "David!"

At first he did not know who had called him, but as he placed his head through the window he practically froze when he saw me.

He apologized profusely for his actions and said, "Don't worry, Sir, I can put you back into business right here." He then proceeded to take his little black book out of his pocket to discuss his business.

"No, no, David," I said, showing him the Bible that lay on the seat next to me. "This is now my little black book, and I am in a far better business than I used to be in."

His eyes opened real wide, and he seemed to be hypnotized by the words "Holy Bible."

I told him about Jesus and invited him to the green tent. I looked at the man I once despised, and as tears came to his eyes and mine, I told him that I loved him. He promised that he would come to the tent.

He hurriedly departed and I doubted whether he would keep his promise.

He didn't.

During my stay in Welkom the pastor from Klerksdorp had gone to my hometown to perform a marriage ceremony. One of those who attended was my wife. She approached the pastor and asked whether he had seen me. He laughed and said, "You had better believe it, Mrs. Rubenstein."

She was puzzled by this remark and said, "He sure must be busy selling furniture because I have not heard from him for close to a month now."

"He is no longer busy in the furniture business, he is now busy in God's business," the pastor informed. She was stunned by this information.

When I arrived home, I confirmed what the pastor had already told her. She had nothing to say in the matter apart from, "I hope that you know what you are doing."

After being home a week we received a telephone call from the manager of the Barclay's Bank. He asked me to come to his office. My wife and I looked at each other. What could he want?

I went to see the bank manager. He advised me that our

account had been overdrawn and showed me the last few checks I had made out to religious organizations. I was not surprised that we were now in the red.

When I got back to the office my wife said, "The manager of the Volkskas Bank wants you."

The first bank manager who had sent for me was from the English bank, now the one from the Dutch bank was looking for me. I left in a hurry, before my wife could ask me about the English bank.

The Dutch bank manager gave me a duplicate of what I had already received. He also showed me some of the checks depicting donations that I had made to various churches.

I walked into our store and my wife could see that I was not going to give her good news. She sat and waited.

I began to tell her about a church that I was in that wanted to sink a well for water. "They did not have the money so I gave them the money."

She stared at me horrified.

"The last church I was in wanted an organ so badly, dear," I told her, but before I could continue with my story she shouted, "So you gave them the money for the organ!" I told her she was absolutely correct.

For the rest of the week the air between my wife and myself was terribly thick. I did my best to console her by telling her that "God had everything under control." She did not appreciate the remark, and asked when she could expect "God to make his first bank deposit?"

I felt very guilty not knowing what to say and could only mutter, "Trust in the Lord and don't despair, my dear." This made her more furious than ever. I did not add any balm to the wound when I said, "Honey, I'm going to work for God now and I hand in my resignation. You will have to manage the business by yourself, as best as you can."

Before she could reply I walked out of the store and went home to decide what my next move would be in "the vineyard of the Lord."

That evening as we were enjoying a well-prepared supper, the telephone rang. It was a pastor who lived 100 miles away. He told me that he was in a revival and that there were many English-speaking people who were attending the meetings. He explained that he did not speak English too well as he was more accustomed to preaching in Dutch.

I told him I had just arrived home and that I thought it better to leave the invitation for a while, and come to him at a later date. I noticed my wife listening to every word and waving her hand toward me. She told me not to refuse the invitation and that she would like to accompany me to that meeting. I told the pastor I would be there the following evening.

We loaded our three girls into the back of the car and took off for the meeting. It was a hot and soggy day. As we passed through a small town the girls decided they would love to have some ice cream. We stopped at a cafe and the girls and I got out of the car. I invited my wife to accompany us but she refused.

After we had enjoyed the ice cream we returned to the car where I found my wife weeping uncontrollably. I could not understand why she was in this condition, and did not ask but drove on.

We arrived at the church and were all heartily welcomed. I noticed my wife took the pastor aside and spoke to him.

I addressed a large audience that evening. At the conclusion the pastor came forward and said, "Friends, please do not leave, we are now about to have an emergency baptism service." I asked who the candidate was and he replied, "You will be surprised."

I was more surprised than he thought I would be when I recognized that the lady walking down the center aisle in a spotless white gown, her hands raised high in the air weeping and praising God, was none other than my wonderful wife.

We returned home the happiest family in the world. We talked, we laughed, we sang, and at times we would just weep for joy.

A new world had now opened for us, and Almighty God had done the opening.

Chapter Seven
Sheep Find a Shepherd

I began to hold tent meetings in and around the city of Johannesburg. One evening I felt impressed to leave the tent prior to my message. Walking outside I found a young man standing there. "Brother Hymie, my congregation has been fasting and praying for you to come and pastor our church," he said. I replied with a loud laugh, and informed him that I was not a pastor but an evangelist. He asked me to consider the invitation, which I promised to do, knowing full well that this could not possibly transpire.

A few days later I received a letter from the church committee inviting me to pastor their flock. I was about to file the letter when something or someone spoke to my heart telling me to accept the call. This puzzled me as pastoring was not in my thinking. However, after accepting I had no doubt in my mind that I had once again heard the voice of the Shepherd.

I went to the church, and after much consultation decided to help them for "the following six months, until you find a pastor." It was four and a half years later that I resigned. During that time the congregation had been gathering twice a week in a hall that was being used by a Boxing Association. Every Saturday night after the Boxing Tournament they would tear down the ring and prepare it for a church platform. I held one meeting there and made up my mind that it would be my first and my last in that place. Driving home from that hall I passed a large vacant single-story building. I brought the car to a sudden standstill, jumped out and tried to look inside the building through windows that were so covered with dirt that it was impossible to see through. I walked to the back of the building and found a window that had been broken. I opened the window and perched myself on the ledge. I looked into a dark building that was littered with dirt. I was afraid to jump down knowing that I would dirty my suit. I decided if I wanted to inspect the place more fully I would have to jump down. As I landed in a heap of dirt I felt Someone say to my heart: "This is my ark." I climbed back out of that window, closed it and inquired from the neighbor about the ownership of the building.

I eventually found the Jewish owner. He was interested in renting the building but wanted to know about my intended use of it. I told him that I wanted to use it to "work for God." He thought it a good idea, so we arranged for a long lease, with an option to buy. I contacted whomever I could of the congregation and told them what I had done, as well as what I was in need of.

The following day practically the whole congregation arrived at what was once a factory and began cleaning operations. Others arrived with trucks to carry away debris. For weeks men, women and children toiled to get the place clean. Once it was clean we decided to paint and never returned to the boxing hall. I had an extra large sign painted and mounted outside the building: "The Ark."

God honored the congregation for their sincerity. There were men and women who prayed daily. There were others who fasted daily. The choir thoroughly enjoyed the rehearsals and their performances. God was in heaven and all was right in The Ark.

I went on a Thanksgiving fast and fasted forty days and forty nights. I had fasted periodically prior to this, but this was my longest fast. I drank water during the fast, and although I became extremely weak and dropped from 210 pounds in weight to 165 pounds, the miracles that took place in The Ark during that time were innumerable. One Sunday morning service as I sat on the platform I was amazed to see people practically fighting to get into the place. Many of the surrounding churches were our best advertisement. Ministers were condemning me for what was taking place in The Ark. Some were forbidding their members to attend the services. Some were sending out threatening letters and others were excitedly preaching about the Apostle Peter and the Apostle Paul, and concluding by warning their members

"Do not go down to that Jew man in The Ark for he is a trickster." Many came to see what "the trickster" was doing and got saved.

One thing that I did learn when I started my ministry as a pastor in The Ark was humility. There were six latrines on the side of the building. Three for Adam, and three for Eve. They were in a most disgraceful state. The factory had been closed for a number of years and many passers-by had used those latrines and forgotten to flush them. The sight of them nauseated me. I tried to find some poor individual around the streets to come and clean them. They could usually be found to do one or two odd jobs. But this day I could not find one. I mentioned the situation to some of the church members, but none were willing to do the job. I felt in my heart that if I were not willing to do it, how could I possibly expect someone else to do it?

After much thought and consideration one evening when nobody knew where I was, I humbled myself and did a job that was most distasteful to me. When I left the six latrines were spotless and ready for use.

News of The Ark had spread to other cities, hospitals, nursing homes and prisons. One missionary called me on the phone one day and explained that he had promised a young lady in the Springs Nursing Home in the city of Springs to ask me to go to her immediately. He explained that her baby had died and that she would not allow them to move the body until I had prayed for the child. This was a great challenge, and I thought it only correct that as this missionary had made a promise that I should go. On my arrival at the hospital I was met at the top of the stairway by the mother. After I introduced myself she held me tightly by the hand and wept, telling me that the doctors had told her that her baby girl had died, and that she would not accept the death of the baby. I sympathized with her, but she refused to accept my sympathy, and asked if I would just go in and pray for the child, telling me that once upon a time Jesus went into the house of a Jewish man by the name of Jairus who was the ruler of a Jewish synagogue. "He raised that young girl from the dead," she reminded me. I asked one of the nurse's permission to go into the room, and she in turn called the Matron. The Matron was most annoyed and mumbled something about "What a lot of rubbish." I told her that I would appreciate her cooperation. She flatly refused to cooperate and called for the doctor. The doctor eventually arrived and he was more bombastic than the Matron, trying to assure me that what the Matron had said was precisely what he had to say—"What a lot of rubbish." Nevertheless he saw that with or without his permission I intended to satisfy the mother. He then shouted at me, "Why don't you run through the whole hospital and heal all the sick?" I said, "Doctor, if Jesus would tell me to run through the hospital I would run through the hospital and Jesus would heal everyone."

The Matron brought me a long white jacket and a white cap and a white mask. She threw them at me and demanded, "You have to put these on so that they will cover you and protect you from any sickness or disease." I tossed the stuff at the nurse standing next to me and said, "I don't need this to cover me and keep me from sickness and disease. I am covered with the precious blood of Jesus Christ of Nazareth."

Without any further ado, I walked into the room and there spotted a nurse standing next to a small black case. It had the shape of a dome. I stood next to her and looked down at what I knew to be the lifeless body of a naked baby girl. I waited and again God moved me. I laid my hands on the glass dome and prayed a prayer of faith. The young nurse was surprised to see this action for she had already asked me if I was the doctor. After a few minutes I opened my eyes and heard the nurse next to me weeping. She said in Dutch, "Ag, my God!" (which in English means, "Oh, my God!")

Nobody had to explain, nobody had to tell me, and nobody had to convince me that there was life in that body that had begun to move. The nurse walked out quickly to make her report, and as the Matron came rushing into the room I vacated it.

The mother looked at me, and without saying or doing anything rushed into the room to see what had happened.

I returned home to my study and once again thanked the loving Son of God, Christ Jesus, that He had proven that "greater things shall ye do" was true.

The following Sunday morning as I stood in The Ark bringing a message of deliverance to the congregation, I noticed a lady enter the church wheeling a large pram in front of her. I recognized the lady as the one who had been told about the death of her daughter. I called her to come up to the front. She wheeled that beautiful bright new pram up the ramp to the pulpit. I asked the lady to tell what had happened. She took her baby out of the pram and told the story how the child had "come out of death into life." The reaction of both believers and unbelievers differed slightly. It seemed it was difficult for both to accept the story. As far as I was concerned what the people thought was irrelevant. The main thing was that mother and child were united.

One thing I had prayed much about and desired was to have my wife at my side so that we could both labor together for the Master. My desire was fulfilled and one weekend she and the girls visited me. We decided I should look for a house. I danced a jig and hugged her and my girls and thanked God for once again answering prayer. My wife sold our business in Bloemfontein and I had a house ready for my family to move into. It was strange at first for us to be together in full service, but it was wonderful.

One day one of my members and I decided to take a short walk, and walked toward the City Hall, where we found thousands of people had congregated to attend a political rally. My friend and I stood in the crowd listening to some politicians. As the clock struck the hour of two, the politicians thanked the attendance (which had grown into approximately 12,000 people) for their support. As they closed their meeting I decided to make full use of the public address system, so I hurriedly pushed my way through the crowd to the microphone and said I had some "good news" for them.

The crowd was on the verge of dispersing, but when they heard someone else addressing them they stood still and listened while I told them of the "King of glory, the prince of peace, the giver of life, the answer to every problem, Jesus Christ the only begotten Son of God."

Many of the listeners immediately thought that I had come there in opposition to the other speakers, and some drew their knives, rushing toward the platform to stab me. At the same time the news photographers went wild trying to get snapshots of this unexpected upheaval. I noticed that the people that had rushed to stab me were held back by some invisible force.

It appeared that an unseen fence stood about five yards from me, and these people who were brandishing knives and daggers could not come any closer. They shouted and cursed and used the Lord's name in vain calling me "a dirty beggar." I felt such a compassion for those wild, lost souls. The politicians snatched the microphone out of my hand.

God was not bound by inventions made by man, He placed a P.A. system right inside my chest and I listened to my voice carrying through the streets of the city. After I had continued magnifying the Lord I was accosted by three of the biggest men I had ever seen. The one grabbed hold of my chest, and together they started screaming and asking me where my God was. I did not know what to answer, but one thing I did know: I was at peace with the whole world. The biggest man then pushed his index finger right up my left nostril forcing my head back. The other two screamed at him to knock my head off. I believe that if he would have hit me that was exactly what he would have done. As he was contemplating just where to hit me I took my hand and placed it around his. I could not look at him because my head was pushed back too far but I said, "Sir, if only you knew this Jesus that I have been telling you about." Instantly the man pulled his big finger out of my nose and stepped back from me, snatching his hand out of mine. His friends asked him why he had not hit me. I heard him say, "Come on you guys, let's get out of here, and let's get out of here real quick." I knew who had touched him!

It was then I determined that this was an ideal place to have a meeting. I walked to the City Hall. The man at the door asked me what was my business. I asked him if he had seen what had taken place after the political meeting. He said he did, and that "that lunatic who had tried to

106

start a church there, should be jailed."

I told him that I was that lunatic and that I wanted to see the city clerk.

He backed away and said I would find him somewhere in the building. That was not helpful at all, but I found the city clerk. I explained that I wished to hold an open-air service on the City Hall steps the following afternoon. He said I would have to have permission from the City Council, and that I would have to put it in writing.

I walked out of the City Hall not knowing where I could find somebody to type this necessary application. Suddenly it felt as though somebody stood by my side, although I knew there was no human being there. Whoever it was put his arm around me, and we walked down the stairs. I crossed the road and walked into a building knowing that this person was guiding me. I opened the gates of the elevator, climbed inside and pushed the fourth floor button. I got off on the fourth floor still not knowing what I was doing or where I was going, but I did know that something supernatural was taking place. I walked down the one passage and made a sharp left into another, and as I looked directly in front of me the sign on the windowpane of the door came out of the door and then went back again. I knew that this was the office that I had to go into. I walked into the office. There was a young lady sitting behind a typewriter with a blank sheet of paper in the machine. I told her who I was and what I wanted. She seemed delighted to help me and asked me if I would like the petition in duplicate. After she had finished she gave me the original to sign, placed it in an envelope, and handed me the duplicate copy. I thanked her most heartily for her kind help and cooperation.

"Excuse me, Sir," she said, "but I have done this typing hoping that after you have finished with your open-air service you will come back and tell me about this Jesus." I promised to do so.

The following day I walked into the City Clerk's office and he recognized me. I waved the letter high in the air and he came over and took it from me. He explained that there were other applications before mine piled up on the table before the mayor and other council members, but he said,

"I will place this one right on the top!"

I walked up and down in that large room with my hands in the air loudly praising God. Every typewriter had ceased typing and every typist watched me. About ten minutes later the man returned with my application form: Granted and signed.

"The council has asked me to ask you to please take care that the people do not stand on the flowers," he said. I promised that I would do the best I could to prevent such a thing happening.

I walked to the City Hall steps and people were milling around. My application had been granted to hold a meeting between the hours of noon and 2:00 p.m. I watched the clock on the Post Office which was across the way from the City Hall, and at five minutes to twelve I became afraid. As I looked at everybody so very busy "doing their own thing," I felt that my message was not unnecessary, but unwanted. I also felt that I would do much better by utilizing my strength in my own church than wasting it on a crowd of people who would not listen.

I was convinced that it would be useless and fruitless so I turned and walked away from the top of the steps. As I walked under the leaves of a large palm tree two unseen hands were laid on my chest, and I stopped in my stride. I felt someone say, "Tell them that Jesus saves." After feeling this touch, as well as hearing the voice, I felt such a power come upon me that I could have lifted the Post Office in my left hand and the City Hall in my right hand and crushed them together.

I walked back to where I had been standing at the top of the steps and as I stood there the large clock in the Post Office chimed twelve. I shouted, "Friends, I stand here today to tell you that Jesus saves." For an hour and thirty minutes I preached as I had never preached before, and quoted Scripture after Scripture that I had never read or heard before. The words just came forth. (I remember returning to my study later and checking up on what I had said, and to my surprise the books, verses, and chapters that I heard myself quoting were in the Bible.)

Now there were thirty minutes left. I stood there rather

exhausted after shouting for one hour and a half. A train conductor approached me and said he had been a "severe migraine sufferer." I looked around at the hundreds of people that had gathered as the conductor removed his cap reverently waiting for me to pray for him. I touched him lightly on the forehead, and before I could pray he threw his hands into the air and began to speak with a strange thing is this?" Some brought me handkerchiefs to pray over. I did not understand why they brought these handkerchiefs, as I had never heard of prayer cloths before. I held the hand- kerchiefs in my hand and prayed over them asking God to bless, to heal and to sanctify. One man took his tie off and asked me to pray over the tie as he was going to the hospital to see a friend. He said he believed that if he had his friend hold the tie his friend would be healed.

A heavy-set lady pushed her way through to the front and as she stood before me she explained about the goiter that I could see sticking out on the right side of the neck. She spoke very indistinctly, and with a high-pitched voice. She tried to explain that she used to sing in the church choir but that the goiter had forced her to resign. Her hus- band came and stood next to her, weeping. I could feel that the air round about me was saturated with power, and that Almighty God himself was present to heal. I placed my hand on the goiter and said a quick prayer. The goiter seemed to slip out of my hand. The lady raised her hands in the air and sang, "How Great Thou Art" in a most beautiful voice. Her husband had become so overwrought with joy that he fell to the pavement and rolled into the street. This had the tendency to put a halt to any traffic that was passing by, and a large double-decker bus had to come to a standstill. The passengers began leaning out the window to see what had happened. This gave me an opportunity to explain that Jesus the Son of God could save from the uttermost to the gutter- most.

Suddenly, I saw the police van arrive, and about ten policemen jumped out. They were led by a sergeant who pushed his way through the crowd. They all had "batons" and when the sergeant came through the crowd he stopped in front of me. It looked as though he had turned to stone.

He could not move. I took a few steps towards him and said, "Sergeant, do you know this lovely Son of God, Jesus Christ of Nazareth?"

He removed his large helmet, and I saw his eyes fill with tears as he said, "Yes, Sir, I know him as my personal Saviour." He then turned about sharply and returned to the transport that had brought him. His followers followed him back into the van and they drove away.

The front page news the following day mentioned the "man that has 'The Ark' in Boksburg North." The advertisements that the magazine companies, as well as the newspaper companies, were giving me was all that I needed to keep me busy both inside and outside the church.

The Jewish people in the area began to pay attention to what was happening and when they would gather at parties they would refer to me as the *mashumed* (the madman).

Chapter Eight
Sowing Seeds of Life

Early one morning I was surprised to receive a long distance telephone call from a farmer friend of mine in Rhodesia. I was even more surprised when the caller asked me when I intended to visit the Holy Land. I told him that I had never intended such a visit, and that there was much expense involved.

"As I walked in my lands this morning praising God, He told me to send you to the Holy Land," my friend advised me. (For the moment I just sat in my study dumbfounded. Then I recalled being informed that there was a large worldwide convention being held in Jerusalem, and thought how nice it would be to visit my sister who lived in Tel-Aviv.)

"That would be real good," I replied, scarcely believing what I had been told.

"Make all the necessary arrangements and I will be there to pay for your ticket in three days time."

I wanted to make further inquiries about the offer, but the caller had replaced the receiver.

I began thinking of the thrill it would be to walk where my Master walked, to talk where my Master talked, to see what He saw, and to hear what He heard. I thought about the wonderful opportunity I would have to win my sister to the Lord Jesus Christ. . . to tell her that Jesus of Nazareth was the Yeshua Hamashiach.

Many friends waved me farewell at the Jan Smut's Airport in Johannesburg, and one lonely figure stood at the Lod Airport in Tel-Aviv waving me a hearty welcome—my sister. We cried and laughed and kissed all at the same time. It had been many years since I had last seen her. Her husband then drove us to their small apartment. In comparison to the large beautiful home that they had been used to in Pretoria, South Africa, I wondered how they could have forfeited all that they had to settle in such a small place. To forsake a flourishing and prosperous cycle business and become farmers on a *kibbutz* (communal farm) also surprised me very much.

One afternoon my sister explained how they had felt the definite leading of God for them to settle in the Holy Land. "You know, Hymie," she said, "wherever one walks here in Israel there is always that feeling that God himself walked here. It feels so very holy."

I quickly agreed and thought that it was now a wonderful opportunity to tell her all about the Great Deliverer and Healer that walked the highways and byways of Israel and the shores of Galilee.

"Mary," I said, "it was not God himself that walked here, but He came in the form of man, and that man was Jesus Christ of Nazareth who was crucified at Calvary that we might all have eternal life."

In a sudden outburst of screaming and yelling she seemed to have lost all control of herself and grabbed the kitchen chair. For a moment I thought that she would strike me with it. She just stood there and gazed at me as though I had committed an unforgivable crime. She then told me that if I had come all that way from South Africa to upset her she would be most happy to see me leave as soon as possible.

I left the following day, never realizing that a seed had been sown in my little sister's heart. Nine years later I had proof of this. I received a letter from Mary asking me to pray for her husband who was dying because of cancer in the stomach. She asked me to "pray in that Name," and although she did not mention the Name, but had put a long dash across the page, I was thrilled to know that the Jesus seed that I planted remained in good ground.

As I walked into the large Convention Hall in Jerusalem I noticed that thousands of believers from across the world had come together. It thrilled me and I took my seat under the banner marked "South Africa." After a few speakers had explained the purpose of the convention they announced that there would be a one-hour break. This gave me time to make the acquaintance of the other South Africans, as well as many others from around the world. The feeling of one big happy family coming together prevailed. I felt so wonderful, and thought that if this was just a little bit of heaven, what was heaven itself going to be like? Some were singing, others were praying for one another, while others were talking all about their journeys and the future plans that they had made to visit the places where Jesus himself had visited. Excitement ranged very high.

About the third day of the convention I hurried down to the old city of Jerusalem. I was like a child as I slowly walked along the Via Dolorosa (the way of the cross) thinking of how the lonely Nazarene had walked that same way himself. As I looked up at the Ecce Homo Arch I thought about the hundreds of scribes and Pharisees that had looked up screaming, "Crucify Him. Crucify Him." I kneeled in the Upper Room, and thanked God for the power He had poured out on those that had tarried there. A tourist stopped me at the bottom of the Upper Room stairway and asked me what had actually taken place there. It was a thrill for me to tell him.

I was blessed as I stood at the Wailing Wall praying for the many friends that I had promised to pray for, but I was twice blessed as I kneeled down in the sepulchre at Gordon's Garden Tomb and thanked the Saviour that the tomb was now empty.

The following morning at the convention I felt "high on the Rock." I noticed a tall heavy-set blonde young man walking aimlessly around the entrance hall of the building. He did not speak to anyone, and I was sure that he was a total stranger. I walked up to him and asked whether he would like to listen to my testimony? He gave me a very warm smile and a very heavy handshake as we relaxed in two arm-chairs that stood nearby. He began to tell me about himself and his wealth, and that he lived in the State of Indiana in the United States of America. He placed much emphasis on his citizenship. After a while he signaled to me that he had said his little bit, and was now prepared to hear what I had to say.

He became particularly interested when I mentioned the time in my life that I had been deeply involved in the diamond smuggling racket. He then motioned for me to stop, and looking around quickly said, "Do you know that is exactly what I am doing here right now in Israel?"

He laughed at me when I told him that Jesus was a *pearl of great price* worth more than diamonds. He tried to keep the subject on illegal diamond buying and selling, but I adamantly hung on to "redemption through the blood of the Lamb."

As we sat there I looked down a long passageway and saw a sign protruding out of the wall: PRAYER ROOM. I asked my American friend to take a walk with me. He agreed, and as we walked he told about the fact that he was on his way to Greece to dispose of a parcel of uncut stones. As soon as we got in line with the Prayer Room I pushed the door open with my right hand, and pulled the young man in with my left hand.

He looked around inside and said, "There is no 'John' here." I closed on his arm with my other hand and looked at him and said, "Please, kneel down here with me." Before he could even think to refuse I fell to my knees pulling him down with me.

I encouraged him to accept God's only begotten Son. To my surprise he did not try to pull away from the firm grip I had on his arm, but instead looked up and said, "Jesus, if you are what this guy says you are, prove yourself to me."

I did not know what the young man felt, but I do know that God answered that prayer instantaneously. I left him on his knees loudly repenting, and begging to be forgiven. I knew in my heart that "there was a new name written down in Glory."

I walked as it were on "cloud number nine" toward the auditorium. Somebody brushed by me. It was a Jewish man wearing a small white covering on his head. He was limping very badly and had a pronounced stoop. I noticed a man walk up to him and say, "My name is Demos Shakarian, and I am the President of the Full Gospel Businessmen's Fellowship International."

Then a priest joined them and said, "I am a priest in the Episcopalian Church."

The limping man looked at both of them. He seemed to

become afraid as the two men joined him. I stood there and watched as they laid hands on the man and began praying for him. I heard the priest say, "Jesus is back in town, brother." Two minutes later that man broke out of that huddle like a champion quarterback. He wasn't carrying a ball, but a complete healing in his body. The stoop had completely gone and the limp had left with it! I looked up toward heaven and said, "Truly, Jesus is back in town!"

I returned home to my congregation. It was good to be back home again, and my friends enjoyed hearing about the wonderful experiences I had in the Holy Land. Many tears were shed as I reminded them about what had taken place in Gethsemane where Jesus cried out, "Nevertheless—Thy will be done."

I was asked to hold a series of meetings close to the Groot Schuur Hospital. This was the hospital where Dr. Christian Barnard had given the first heart transplant. Mr. Blaiberg was his patient. I told my first audience that Dr. Christian Barnard thought that he was the first one to give a heart transplant but that I had been giving heart transplants long before him, "with the help of the Holy Ghost." We all enjoyed that humor.

One evening as I was about to deliver the message a man walked down the center aisle with something that looked like a guitar. It looked as though it was fit for the trash can. He explained that he wanted permission to sing.

I replied that I had a group of singers that he had already heard, plus a wonderful choir that he had already heard, and that I felt that we had already had sufficient singing. I looked at the man's attire. It appeared to me as though he had just crawled out from under a tractor. The man ignored what I told him and turned about and hollered for somebody else to join him. A lady joined him, and she looked as though she had also climbed out from under a tractor. Her clothing was badly in need of both repair and cleaning. I could see that they were going to sing regardless. They walked to the end of the platform up the stairs and came and stood right next to me at the pulpit. I wondered what effect this would now have on the fully-packed hall.

It seemed to me that the more they tried to get their

broken-down guitars into tune, the more they got out of tune. They began to sing an old-time religious song, and they had scarcely finished the first verse when the total audience stood to their feet. Many were crying, many were praying and many were praising God. I looked up towards heaven and asked God to forgive me for condemning the two singers. Once again I was taught a lesson by the Holy Ghost who had come to teach His children many lessons.

After a long while silence was once again resumed and I continued with the message. The Lord was truly present and there was much power to do mighty miracles. As usual, I invited the needy to come forward for prayer. The response was terrific. Hundreds stood around the hall, and I began to pray for each one individually. As I walked to one young man he handed me his spectacles. They were done up neatly in a smart celluloid case. I did not know what he wanted and asked him why he had given me his spectacles.

"God told me if you would break these that He would restore perfect eyesight to me," the young man replied.

I was reluctant to do what he expected me to do, so I tried to hand back the case to him. He refused to take it and said, "Please, break them, sir, for I believe God."

This was something entirely new to me, and I did not know what procedure to adopt, but as I looked at the hundreds who were waiting for prayer I broke both the case and the spectacles and pressed them into the hands of the man.

The following day the young man was practically unable to see a thing. He managed to drive to his work at the railroad station office. He believed that it was only the grace of God that helped him to drive back to his house after work.

The following day the young man was totally blind. He called his wife and asked her to please drive him to work. He explained that he could not see. His wife cried and said much about the fact that I had broken his spectacles. She also reminded him of all the money they had spent to purchase them.

He insisted that she drive him to work and help him to get to his office desk. They got to the office early so that nobody would see the predicament the young man was in. He sat at his desk and felt for both pencil and paper, and as the rest of the staff came in and greeted him he returned their salutations, and pretended to be busy by scribbling on the paper before him. The office manager then walked in and stopped at his desk with, "Good morning, young Jannie, I see that you are not wearing your glasses today."

Jannie stood and looked toward the voice that had spoken and then said, "Sir, I do not need my glasses any longer because two nights ago a Jewish man prayed for me and Jesus Christ gave me a pair of new eyes." Instantly God gave the young man a pair of perfect new eyes.

I later examined the young man's eyes and had never seen a more beautiful, bright, pale-blue set of eyes in my life.

After the series of meetings I was happy to return to The Ark once again. I found that in my absence God had continued blessing more than ever. My friends said in good humor, "Brother Hymie, things go better when you are away."

It was now eighteen months since I had done my first forty-day fast, and now I decided to do a second one. This time I did not work as hard as I did the previous time.

After the first five days I drank a glass of warm water with a tablespoon of salt and that cleaned my stomach out entirely. I was now ready to continue for the remainder of the fast without much difficulty. The problem arose when I was coming out of the fast. It was more difficult to come out of the fast than it was to get into the fast. It seemed that somebody had caught me in a vice and was trying to squeeze the life out of me. I did not know what this sudden seizure was, but I knew that the long fast had brought it about. I walked into the living room where my wife was and motioned to her to take me to the hospital.

As I lay in the back of the car certain that I would not reach the hospital, I began to smell the soil of the earth. Somehow I knew that my day of reckoning had come, but I prayed, "Dear God, I have a peace in my heart and I am not afraid to die. But if there is anything that I have left undone I would appreciate it very much if you would show me what I failed to do."

In a split second God showed me places and people I

117

had not witnessed to. He also showed me people that had not been healed. He showed me multitudes of people running over a cliff and plunging to their death into eternal darkness. I knew that in many instances I had failed God.

Upon arrival at the hospital I was rushed into the emergency room and the doctor who tried to interrogate me became most annoyed because I could only answer his questions in a strange tongue that neither he nor I understood. I was given all manner of injections and tubes were stuck into my right hand, as well as in my nose. My wife tried to explain that the cause of this attack was due to "a forty-day fast," but none of the medical staff understood what she said.

Slowly I began to recover. In spite of witnessing people dying practically daily in the large ward in which they had placed me with twenty other patients, I still continued to recover.

Each afternoon at visiting time between 20 to 30 of my congregation would come to visit me. They would gather around the bed and one by one they would tire me by asking questions. When the warning bell would ring for visitors to leave the elders would come to the head of the bed and lay hands on me (not too gently). They would then pray for me and shake me very roughly. Some would shout, "Come out of him, devil." I thought that if there were any in me they would most surely be shaken out of me.

Shortly after this procedure the doctor would come around on his usual inspection and say that he was very puzzled that I was so well in the morning and so run down in the afternoon. I explained to him about the good intentions of some of my church members, but that their actions were not helping me to recover. The doctor was surprised and agreed that they were hindering my complete recovery. I asked the doctor if it was possible to put me into a private ward where I was sure I could have a lot better time of relaxation without seeing people die daily, as well as a large group of prayer warriors visiting me. He agreed and had me moved into a semi-private ward.

The only difference in that place was that I did not see the dead taken away, but the prayer warriors arrived daily, on time, and continued commanding devils to come out of me and practically shaking what life I had in me, out of me.

The doctor was far from satisfied with my progress, and although I did not intend to complain any further, he placed me in a private ward and had a large sign placed on the door which read: VISITORS STRICTLY FORBIDDEN. This caused an uproar in the church. They felt that this action by the hospital authorities was hindering my recovery as they felt that unless they kept shaking devils out of me I had no chance of recovering.

I fully recovered and returned to continue to pastor the flock. Quite a few of my members asked me why I had had the sign prohibiting visitors. I asked them whether they were not happy that I was now once again fit and strong to tell the world about the Jesus who had healed me after a forty-day fast?

I received a letter from the United States of America. It had been sent by a group called "The World-wide Deliverance Evangelists." In the letter I was asked to visit the United States representing the Deliverance Evangelists of the Republic of South Africa. This was a surprise to me as I had never heard of this organization, and neither did I know any of its members. I felt it an honor to be chosen out of the thousands of men who were being used in the deliverance ministry.

I knew practically nothing about America. I did know that they called their flag, "Old Glory." I also knew that they often spoke about an "Uncle Sam," and that the people spoke "through their noses."

I showed the letter to my wife, and without hesitation she said, "Honey, I think that you should go." I laughed aloud, knowing full well that I did not have the necessary finances to go. For a while I tried to put the thought of going out of my mind. But each day that I would talk to the "King of glory" I felt so impressed to reply to the letter that I would accept the invitation.

I told my wife I would "put out a fleece." "Honey, if my daddy, who is a prosperous Jewish business man, will

119

give me the money to go to the United States of America I will take this as a definite confirmation from God that He wants me there."

We arrived at my father's hotel, sat down, spoke a while and then I handed him the letter that I had received. He read it and handed it back to me, and suggested that it would be a good idea for me to go.

I explained that I was unable to go as I did not have the necessary money.

Without hesitation he said, "That's all right, my boy, I will give you the money."

I said, "Dad, do you know what I will be doing in the United States of America?"

He did not answer me so I continued, "I will be praying for people in the name of Jesus. I will be telling people about Jesus who I believe is the Son of God. I will preach the New Testament to thousands." And as I was about to continue to tell him what I was going to do he raised his voice and said, "Did I ask you what you were going to do?"

Chapter Nine
Land of the Free

I called a special church board meeting and asked for permission to go to the United States. There was a division on the board. Some were in full agreement and others were not. I explained that I felt the Holy Spirit compelling me to go. The division remained as some understood what I was talking about but others did not. I decided that we should all make it a matter of prayer and assemble again in three days.

During the three days I felt strongly impressed to hand in my resignation and leave my congregation and feel completely free. At the next meeting the division remained so I put everyone's mind at ease by handing in my resignation. There was no division any longer, and with tears in their eyes they asked me to reconsider. I told them that I had now made up my mind as I was not sure whether I could put a definite dateline on my ministry and promise to return at a certain time.

I was given a big farewell party, and probably 200 people brought me a prophecy assuring me that I was entirely out of the will of God. I was more than positive that the prophets were not prophesying too well. The more they prophesied the more I felt the drawing to the United States.

As hundreds stood in the air terminal singing, "God be with you till we meet again," I walked out of the terminal toward the large Pan American aircraft that stood there waiting to take me to the U.S.A. As I got to the top of the stairway to enter the plane, I turned around and waved to my congregation that I was now leaving forever. Hankies were being waved by both prophets and false prophets.

A sweet American air hostess smiled at me and said through her nose, "Welcome aboard, Sir, we are glad to have you fly with us to the United States of America." That welcome put new pep into my heart and I knew that from there on I would not only love the American people but I would also love their country.

After a long tiresome flight, which covered about 10,000 miles, having stopped at Leopoldville, we flew over the great city of New York. Manhattan looked like a great big beautiful fairyland. We landed at the Kennedy International Airport, and people were buzzing about like busy buzzing bees.

I had no difficulty getting through the customs and was welcomed by my wife's sister and family. New York was exactly what they had told me New York would be. A great big city with high skyscrapers and many people.

I stayed with my sister-in-law's family in an apartment on Clinton Avenue in Brooklyn.

The first morning directly after breakfast Larry, my wife's brother-in-law, got me all excited about seeing New York. I noticed that everybody seemed to be excited and very nervous, and what seemed to be "in high gear." No sooner did we leave the apartment and get on the sidewalk than Larry hurried away. He turned to me and shouted, "Come on, man, in this country you've got to get with it." I gathered that he was telling me to get into "high gear."

I practically had to run to keep up with him, and noticed that everybody seemed to be in a rush. When I asked him to slow down a bit, he laughed at me and said, "You're in America now, get into the rat race."

I was tired when we climbed the stairway leading to a train track that had been erected above the street. The train arrived and we jumped in together with another thousand people. They bumped and pushed, and I disliked it immensely. We arrived somewhere in downtown New York, and without asking for any assistance whatsoever, the crowd practically carried me off the train, down the stairway onto the sidewalk. I searched around for Larry hoping that I had not lost him. He came to me, grabbed me hastily by the arm, and together we rushed down another stairway into the underground subway. Trains kept flying by. He said they were traveling at perhaps 100 miles an hour. I suggested that we get a cab to wherever we were going, but a train stopped right in front of us as I made the suggestion and the doors opened wide. I had no intention of being left behind so I took a wild jump into the train alongside my guide.

I took a firm grip on a piece of leather that was hanging down from the ceiling and hoped that the journey would be a safe one. "The next stop we jump for it," Larry said quickly. The high gear and excitement that was upon him was now upon me, and I was all ready to jump for it when the train stopped. It stopped, the doors opened and I jumped. We rushed up the stairway again onto another sidewalk and then we arrived at the ferry that was to take us across to the Statue of Liberty. I was so exhausted at that time that I could scarcely walk onto the ferry. Larry laughed and told me that he was sure I would be "acclimatized" and strong in the next few days.

When we arrived at the Statue of Liberty Larry suggested that we take the elevator to the top. I was thrilled when we found that the elevator was "out of order." Larry was upset about this but promised to bring me back another time. I said nothing to his proposal but knew in my heart that this was both the first and the last time that I'd be visiting any place with Mr. Larry Dooner.

When we returned to the mainland he flagged down a taxi. He told the driver to take us to the Empire State Building. I told him that I was both tired and hungry, and suggested that we do more visitation the following day. He said there was a restaurant in the building and that we could also relax for a time. We had to stand in a long line before we were able to get into the elevator to go up to a certain level. When we got to the level I was thankful that we were there. I wanted to sit down and relax, but Larry said, "Come, and look on the outside."

I walked outside and beheld a most fantastic scene. The many ships in the Hudson River, the many buildings and the many cars just thrilled me, but it did not take away my fatigue and hunger.

I walked back into the building intending to relax when Larry took me once again by the arm and said, "There is still a higher level." This was bad news for me. Once again we stood in a line waiting to get into another elevator that would take us to the higher level. I was now exhausted, as we walked around the outside on that higher level. I kept telling my guide how tired I was, but he kept ignoring me saying, "Isn't it too wonderful for words!"

I do not remember how we returned to the apartment, but I do remember collapsing on my bed and falling sound asleep. Early the following morning Larry was busy shaking me. "Come on, Hymie," he said, "today I will show you many, many more interesting things here in New York."

I shouted at him, "Buddy, go and show them to yourself." I pulled the blankets over my head and fell asleep as I heard the family laughing at my refusal to leave with him.

A few days later I was traveling along on the Greyhound bus heading for the "motor city" of Detroit. Upon my arrival I made inquiries about finding the YMCA.

The following day was the first day of the convention, and I walked from my room down Woodward Avenue to the large Cobo Hall. It was a lot quieter than walking along Lexington Avenue in Manhattan. The shops were also very attractive but the people did not seem to have that "high gear" that they had in New York City. Hundreds of people had gathered in the Cobo Hall; I introduced myself to many of them. There were evangelists from practically every country in the world. This thrilled me as I had not met many evangelists outside of South Africa. There were many testimonies from various parts of the world, but all focused on the Lamb of God who was the "Great Physician of our time."

I was allotted time to speak one afternoon at two. One of the committee members approached me and said, "Brother Hymie, we have been trying to contact you in the hotel, but we were unable to. Where are you staying?"

I felt rather embarrassed to tell him where I was staying, as everyone else was staying in a most luxurious hotel a few blocks away from the Cobo Hall. I told him not to be concerned, that I was most comfortable and happy where I was staying. He could see that I was trying to avoid the question and rephrased it for me. When I eventually told him where I was staying he took me by the arm, and in his Cadillac drove to the YMCA, paid for my stay there and loaded all my goods into the luggage box. He then took me to the hotel where he was staying and booked me in. It was a most beautiful hotel room that they had given me.

The first thing I did was pull a switch and watch the television come alive. I was thrilled to see that this one was in color, as the one at the YMCA was only black and white. As there was no television in South Africa I just sat there amazed at what that machine produced. I then noticed there was a price tag behind the door and when I saw the "charges per day" I went faint.

The afternoon that had been allotted to me eventually arrived. Although I had no doubt that my Friend would be standing right there by my side, I did feel rather nervous. There were a few preliminaries, singing and testimonies and then the director introduced me. As he did so the public address system ceased to operate. They bumped it, knocked it, and hit it but it still did not operate. Suddenly the general public address system that was connected to every room and hall in the building came into action. "Ladies and Gentlemen," the voice was loud and strong, "we deeply regret that we have cut off other P.A. systems but we have an important announcement." It appeared that the speaker was having difficulty in saying what he had to say. "Friends," he again continued, "I am sorry to inform you that our President, John F. Kennedy, has been shot in the city of Dallas, Texas."

The general P.A. system cut out as hundreds of people began yelling, screaming, crying and embracing one another. I took a seat at the back of the platform, shocked. I had heard of the power that the President of the United States had in the whole wide world, and by the reaction of the people felt that the whole of the convention would be cancelled, and that I would be obliged to return home without having done anything for God in the country.

I could hear the general public address system click into operation again, and this time I could clearly hear the announcer weeping. "Dear friends, we have now received further news about our dear President, John F. Kennedy. I regret to announce that our beloved President died on the way to the hospital." Some people sat there frozen in their seats, including myself. Others were too dumbfounded to say anything as they stood and stared at each other. I heard the P.A. system in the hall click on.

The chairman very wisely and very quietly called the gathering to order. This took quite a while, but when everybody stood silently the chairman said, "Friends, let us pray for the soul of our late President, and for his loved ones and family. Also, let us pray for this nation that Almighty God will keep His mighty hand upon it." He then led the congregation in the "Lord's Prayer," and then prayed for the President and the country. This brought about a spirit of tranquility and the song leader came forward and led the gathering to sing, "There is Power in the Blood." By the time we finished singing the song over and over the assassination of the President had been temporarily forgotten. With that the chairman came to me and told me to take over the service.

I introduced myself and explained how sorry I was about the assassination. I talked a while about my friend Jesus, the Christ of Nazareth. I felt impressed that there were five people who could be, and should be saved, immediately.

"Friends," I said, "I am doing what I feel I should be doing. The Holy Ghost has instructed my heart that there are five people who wish to be saved right now. Would those five people kindly come forward immediately that we might pray together, and accept Jesus Christ as their personal Lord and Saviour?"

From certain portions of the hall four people came forward. They wept as they stood there. The crowd of approximately 800 people raised their hands to heaven and thanked the Lord that "He was still in the saving business." I waited for the fifth person to come but there was no response. I looked into the crowd and about fourteen rows from the front, sitting five seats off the left-hand aisle I could scarcely see the lady who was sitting there in a bright red dress. I pointed to her and said, "That lady in the red dress sitting about fourteen rows from the front and on a seat about five seats away from the left-hand aisle, you are the fifth person."

That lady jumped up screaming and ran to the front, and admitted that she was the fifth person. She took the microphone from me and said, "Friends, twenty-one years ago I felt that the Lord would want me to do missionary work in the Far East. All this time I made one excuse after another why I could not go. Three days ago I received this brochure of this convention," she said, holding up the brochure high above her head. "I opened it to the page where there are over 100 small snapshots of the evangelists who would be coming to this convention. I noticed the snapshot of this man," she said as she pointed to me. "This man from South Africa. I told God that if this man would point me out in the crowd and ask me to come forward, I would know my place was to work for God in the Far East."

People clapped hands and thanked God that "the gift of knowledge" had not died.

The lady held my hands tightly and thanked me for my obedience. I reciprocated and thanked her for her obedience. The two of us rejoiced that God had spoken to us individually. Together the five people who stood before me lifted their hands to God and in the name of Jesus repented of their sins and dedicated their lives to the King of glory.

I testified like a man who had something to testify about. I quoted the words of Jesus that said, "Go ye into all the world, and preach the gospel to every creature. He that believeth and is baptized shall be saved; but he that believeth not shall be damned. And these signs shall follow them that believe, in my name shall they cast out devils; they shall speak with new tongues; they shall take up serpents; and if they drink any deadly thing, it shall not hurt them."

I told them I had preached the gospel, and now I was about to do the last thing that Jesus said to do, "They shall lay hands on the sick, and they shall recover." The sick began to come forward. It appeared to me that everyone there was sick. I instructed them to stand in rows in the aisles, two rows in each aisle (which made eight long rows) of sick and lame.

I jumped off the platform and with both arms extended began to walk up the first aisle touching each one individually. Faith was running so high at this point that as I walked to pray for people they were already testifying to their healings. I was so happy I had come to the Cobo Hall in the motor city of Detroit in the United States of America.

That night I could not attend the meeting as I was totally exhausted. I was told that the chairman had made an announcement and apologized for the Jewish man from South

127

Africa who had taken a little longer time than had been allotted him. Everybody clapped and thanked God as the chairman concluded by saying, "But it most certainly was worth it all."

The following morning after once again studying the price tag at the back of the door I went to the Cobo Hall without breakfast. I did not intend fasting, but I realized that it would be a lot cheaper to fast.

As I walked inside the hall one of the men came to me and handed me an envelope saying, "The committee wants you to have this small token of appreciation." I hurriedly opened the envelope and was happy to see a check for $200. I had not been promised any money to speak, neither was I promised any money to assist in my traveling expenses. But that $200 was like candy to a little boy. I felt so happy now that I could meet my commitments, and could live like the others lived in that "flashy, splashy hotel."

I joined the other evangelists on the platform, and once again the hall filled to capacity. The speaker that morning was a man from Dallas, Texas. I could see that he was well experienced by the way he addressed himself to the large audience. He apologized and said that he felt very sorry about the fact that President Kennedy was killed in his city. He then had everyone stand and sing, "God Bless America." I did not know the words but I joined in as best I could, and cried as loud as the loudest.

The speaker told about his large printing work, as well as his large mailing list. He told of the thousands of books that he had distributed throughout the world. He told of experiences that he had had in different parts of the country and in various parts of the world. He thrilled me, and I know that he thrilled hundreds of others as he told how he witnessed thousands baptized during one prayer, in the "Holy Ghost period." He hesitated for quite a while and then said, "Friends, this same Holy Ghost who spoke to Simon Peter as he lay on the roof of a building, and told him that there were visitors to see him has spoken to my heart and told me that there are thirty people who are to give $200."

There was a quick response by some, but others seemed to hesitate. After a while he counted twenty-nine who had

128

responded and said, "Number thirty, please come quickly that I might continue with my message." With the others who sat on the platform we waited for number thirty to come forward, but there was apparently no number thirty in the crowd. I felt a small soft voice speak to my heart and say, "You are the man." I sat there frozen in my seat. I wondered how I could possibly be the man. Then it dawned on me that as I sat there, there was a check in my pocket for $200. *Surely the good Lord would not expect me, who was probably the poorest financially in that gathering, to give to that man who had more than I had, everything that I now possessed financially,* I thought. The anointing broke the yoke and I walked off the platform weeping uncontrollably as I handed the evangelist the check that had been given to me only an hour previously.

That evening one of the American evangelists told the audience that he felt very impressed to take up a "special offering" for the Jewish evangelist from South Africa.

I felt embarrassed as they placed me on the floor in front of the pulpit and hundreds of people walked by me placing different-sized bills and silver into my hands. It did not take long for my outside jacket pockets to get filled. It did not take long for my inside jacket pockets to get filled. Then my side trouser pockets, and then my back trouser pockets were stuffed with dollar bills. One man unbuttoned the front of my shirt and began stuffing bills into it. Somebody suggested that they "bring the barrel." As I stood there like a stuffed dummy a large barrel was placed at the side of me, and the people began throwing dollar bills and silver into the barrel, and laughing at me as I could hardly move.

That evening we counted the money that had been given to me and $400 were added to the $200 that I had given away that morning. I could only give credit where credit was due, to "the Lamb of Calvary," who once again had proved that He was able to perform over and above that which I could even ask or think.

As I approached my room I noticed that there were a few pieces of paper pinned to the door. I took the papers, unlocked the door and sat on the bed to see what was written. To my surprise, two well-known pastors had arranged for me to spend one week in revival in each of their churches. I sat there crying again, and wondered about "the love of God, and how measureless and strong" it was.

The convention came to a close. I went to the desk clerk to pay my bill. "There is no bill to pay, Sir," the young lady said smiling at me, "it has already been paid." I turned away not knowing whether to scream, shout, or embrace an elderly lady who seemed to be having trouble with her puppy that stood nearby. I pulled out one of the bills from that bundle of $600 and just wanted to once again look at the inscription on it: IN GOD WE TRUST.

The intended six weeks that I was going to spend in the United States extended to six months, and then to twelve months. I was kept busy practically each night and I was thrilled to see that when "God opens doors no man shuts them."

I returned to South Africa via Brussels. In spite of the heavy rainstorm, there were many friends to welcome me back home safely. For the next few weeks I was bombarded with visits from different members, different pastors and different friends. I had four or five churches offered to me, as well as revivals. I accepted a few revivals to keep the "wolf away from the door." Somehow I felt that I had left home. Somehow and in some way I had become "hooked" on America.

My wife said, "Who knows, Hymie, one day we might pack up the girls and take off to that land of milk and money." We laughed at the quotation.

My wife decided to make all the necessary inquiries, should we ever decide to pack up and settle in the land where "Old Glory proudly flies." There was so much red tape attached to the whole affair that at times I told my wife that it would be better and less troublesome to just stay put.

Right after this statement I regretted that I had said what I did. I realized that everything was not served to anyone on a plate. I realized that God had not promised skies always blue, nor did He promise flower-strewn pathways all our life through. I knew that God had not promised the sun without the rain, and neither did He promise peace without sorrow, and joy without pain. I was well aware of the fact

130

that God had not promised that we would not bear many a burden and many a care, but I knew for sure that He had promised strength for the day and rest for the laborer and light for the way.

We began to do what we termed the easy things. We got all the necessary application forms. (There were many of these.) We got forms that were needed to be signed by a doctor, forms to be signed by police authorities, forms to be signed and granted by one authority or another. Slowly, but surely, we began working with the forms.

After a few months we had most of our forms in order, as well as the necessary air travel arrangements. All we needed to complete the air travel arrangements was the money. We discovered that one of our Christian friends had his own travel agency so we paid him a quick visit to find out the cheapest and easiest way for a family of five to fly one way to the United States. The man suggested that if we would care to make the flight and pay later as best we could, he could also arrange that. This interested me. If we were going to fly that would be the only way we could possibly get off the ground.

We considered selling what furniture we could, but when our friends and missionaries came to buy we sold nothing and gave away everything.

I encouraged my wife and our daughters by telling them that "very soon we will be flying to the wonderful United States."

We called upon the American Consulate regularly, and the young girl who attended to us was more than a pleasure to do business with. We agreed upon the day of departure and she said, "Hey, you guys, I forgot to tell you that there are two forms that are missing. The one is the form that has to be signed by your doctor guaranteeing that he has given you a blood examination. The other is the form from the police guaranteeing that you have had no previous police record."

At the mention of the police record my wife looked at me, but I paid no attention. The young lady told us to bring those forms as soon as possible.

As my wife and I walked into the elevator we were both concerned. "I guess we have had it," my wife said to me in a very defeated voice.

The following day we went to the doctor who had our blood tested and issued us a clean bill of health.

We called at the office of the chief of police in Johannesburg. He was very friendly and after we told him about our intentions, he asked my wife her full name, and then said, "I know I don't need to ask you if you have a previous record," and before she could answer he stamped the form with the large word CLEAR, and stamped the police stamp underneath and signed it very boldly.

He took the second form and looked at me and said, "Rev. Rubenstein, I know that I can clear you as well."

"Excuse me, Sergeant," I said to him very slowly as I gazed into his dark-brown eyes. "I have a police record."

He explained that under those conditions it would be impossible for me to settle in the United States of America. He also further suggested that in order to make things a lot easier for me he would simply stamp my form and sign it and clear me so that I could enter into the country.

I explained to the Sergeant that I was a born-again Christian, and as long as I held that title I was going to behave as a born-again Christian.

He instructed me to call back the following day, and he would have a copy of my police record ready for me.

We returned as he had asked us to, and he handed me my police report with a long list of crimes that I had been found guilty of during my court case in Kimberly. As I looked at the list I felt butterflies flying in my stomach.

I knew that Mr. O'Lenick, the American consul, was not going to be too happy about this. The young lady in the office was happy to see us return with our papers. She said that time was running out and that everything was ready for us to go. She looked through my wife's blood test form and then through the police form and said, "Well, honey, you're on your way." (There were three days left for us to fly out.)

Then she took my papers, looked through my blood report quickly and put that on one side, and as she looked through my police report she went pale. She looked up at me inquiringly and then back at the paper. She excused herself as she hurried away to the office of Mr. O'Lenick.

She returned and apparently had lost her happiness on the way. "Mr. O'Lenick would like to see you, Sir," she said.

I walked into the office, and the American consul signaled for me to take a seat. One look at his face, and one look at the signal and I could see that a large barrier had risen between us.

"Is this your police report, Rev. Rubenstein?" he asked.

I replied in the negative.

He looked at the report again and said, "But the name on here is Mr. Hyman Rubenstein."

"Sir," I replied, "that was Mr. Hyman Rubenstein, but this man sitting here before you is Rev. Hyman Rubenstein. Please allow me to explain." I told him that the man who that police report belonged to was dead. That the man now sitting in front of him was a new man, a new creature and not a sinner but a blood-washed saint of God. "Jesus Christ has cleansed me and forgiven me of all my sins and therefore I feel that it would not be fair for you to jeopardize me because of the man I used to be."

It was obvious that the American consul had no idea what I was trying to tell him, instead he made a weak reply, "I will have to contact Washington."

I made sure that he was well aware of the fact that we had made all arrangements to fly out of the country. Then I said, "Sir, it is not Washington that you should contact with regard to me, but God."

The delay lasted for seven months, and for seven months we lived in a way we had never lived before. At times I felt tempted to make application to take on another church, but I knew deep down in my heart that the answer was on the way.

At last I was happy to leave for the United States, and arranged that my wife and the three girls would follow a month later, as all the original plans had been cancelled in the United States. As Mr. O'Lenick, the American consul handed me both my visa and my green card he apologized for the delay. I accepted his apology, and told him that I was only too happy that heaven had come through in my behalf.

This time as the plane left mother earth, and I looked out of the window, I knew that there was no turning back.

Upon my arrival in the United States I made my way to Chicago where another World-wide Convention of Deliverance Evangelists was in progress.

Following the convention an evangelist offered me a revival meeting in Brooklyn, New York, which would be at the same time my wife and girls were to arrive. I readily accepted the invitation.

One of the convention members told me that he had an Oldsmobile car that he was trying to sell. I told him that he was talking to the buyer if he would allow me time to pay for it. He showed me the car and agreed that I could pay him as best I could.

I drove from Chicago to New York very slowly and very carefully. I had placed a large sign on the dashboard and it leaned against the windshield: KEEP RIGHT.

As I crossed over the George Washington Bridge into Manhattan I found myself on the wrong side of the road— African style. With many horns honking and many people shouting I swerved back to the correct side. I turned off the ignition and jumped out of the car and ran into the Hotel Pare that was right where I had stopped. I asked a man at the counter where I was making reservations if he would kindly help me as I was not feeling well, and take the keys to my car and park the car in the place where parking was permissable. The man laughed and informed me that he was not a parking attendant and that two blocks south of the hotel was a large parking area. I was more afraid and more confused than ever.

I had no idea what was south or what was north or what was east or what was west, but I walked out of the hotel and the more I studied the traffic the more I regretted buying the car. I had answered every question that they had asked me at the driver licensing place in Indiana, but I regretted that I had passed the course, as I noticed cop cars and ambulances flying in all directions, with their sirens blowing louder than loud. I got behind the steering wheel, started the engine, and cried to God for help. The car moved slowly, and as I crossed the first intersection I looked down the road and noticed a big neon sign flickering on and off with the word PARKING on it.

I decided to make a right at the next intersection, and had halfway completed the turn when I saw a sign pointing in the opposite direction. I knew that sign, so I pulled the car back onto the road—much to the anger of a taxicab that nearly collided with me. I felt like crying, but I knew that that wouldn't help, so I got to the next intersection. I smiled as I saw a traffic light. I was glad to stop for a while. The light turned green and I made the right turn. Somehow I arrived at the place where the sign had been flickering. I got out and asked the parking attendant where I should put the car, and he took my keys and asked for $5. I was not sure whether he was the parking attendant or not, but I was happy to give him the keys to the car and the $5.

The following morning I phoned my sister-in-law and told her that I was in the city. She was glad to hear from me, and shouted, "Come on over, we are waiting for you." She immediately began explaining how to get to Clinton Avenue from where I was. There were so many turns north, turns south, and turns east that I told her that it would be impossible for me to find the place.

"Don't be silly," she said, "you go to Queen's Bridge and over Queen's Bridge you turn east to Brooklyn Bridge, over Brooklyn Bridge turn west," and so she carried on from one turn to another and from one bridge to another that I told her if she did not quit I would put down the phone.

I decided that it might be wiser for me to have a large enjoyable breakfast before I entered into that parking place. I did feel a lot better after eating and walked to the parking place. The attendant was busy and shouted at me to get my car out of the parking lot quickly as there were others who wanted to come in.

I wanted him to give me some direction as to how to get to Brooklyn. In two seconds he shouted a whole list of instructions and walked away.

I drove out of the parking place into those streets where cars and trucks were literally flying by. I was happy to see a large Gulf service station on the corner. I accelerated the motor and got off the road into the service station. The gas attendant seemed to be as busy as the parking attendant. After he had filled my tank with gas I told him that I needed

135

help and except he help me I would not pay him and he could call the cops. He laughed and said, "You Englishmen are all the same." He had thought that I was from England by my accent.

He was kind enough to draw a map, and I was thrilled when I came to the end of my journey and parked outside the apartment on Clinton Avenue right against a fire hydrant.

As I climbed out of the car somebody shouted from an apartment window, "Hey, you there, that's a fire hydrant."

I hurried into the apartment and received a warm welcome. I was happy to hear Larry singing under the shower. I went to the door and told him to hurry as I had a job for him to do. When he came out of the bathroom I handed him the keys to my car and said, "Buddy, do me a real big favor, please, and take my car away from the fire hydrant outside and dump it in the Hudson River."

Larry parked the car somewhere and came back laughing loudly. I did not deny the fact that I had been terrified driving through Manhattan and through Brooklyn. Later that day Larry showed me the way to the Theater Building that I was to preach in. Once again I drew a map of how to get to the place. I had to drive at night, and that was not very comforting.

The following day I drove to the Theater Building and decided to find accommodations as near to the place as possible so I could walk and not have to drive.

There were no hotels or motels in that area but many apartments. I walked one block, and in desperation walked to the door of an apartment and knocked on the door. An elderly lady answered and spoke to me in Puerto Rican, I think. I tried to explain to her that I was looking for a room. She closed the door in my face.

I knocked again and this time a young Puerto Rican girl stood there. I told her exactly what I had told the lady, and she explained to the lady what I needed. They had a lengthy meeting, and eventually decided that I spoke so easily about Jesus and the meetings that I was holding in the Theater Building that "I was a good fellow." The young girl told me that the lady wanted $15 a week for the upstairs room.

I climbed the stairs and walked into a neat bedroom. It

had a large double bed in it, and that was practically all that it could hold.

A few days later it was time for my family to arrive. By then I had made all inquiries of how to get from the theater to the Kennedy Airport. I was happy to find a parking place at the airport, and even happier as I stood on the balcony and watched the plane from South Africa unload my wife and three girls. I waved at them frantically, but they seemed to be very nervous. They went through customs and then met me in the foyer. As I embraced them and kissed them they seemed to relax. We managed with much difficulty to get ourselves and all our baggage into the car. A short time later I pulled up at the apartment on Clinton Avenue.

There was much excitement and the Rubenstein family was welcomed into the United States of America. Each one of us had arrived at the Kennedy Airport, New York, with forty pounds of baggage, and our hearts full of "Faith in Almighty God."

I had begun to get a steady income from the donations that were collected each night, and with this we were able to buy the strict necessities.

I contacted a friend in Ohio and asked him whether he could arrange services for me in some churches in his area. "Come on over, we are waiting for you," he hollered over the telephone. I had seemed to have heard these words before. I asked him to make some kind of arrangements for us to stay somewhere for a while. He told me that there was nothing to worry about, he would arrange everything.

I felt very sorry for my three girls, but particularly sorry for my wife. In no way were we accustomed to such a life of insecurity. My immovable faith in God made it easy for me. But there were times that I had compassion on my wife who was used to living in a beautiful home under the most comfortable conditions. Now she suddenly found that if she did not do the thing herself it would not be done at all. She had been used to the servants doing everything.

We arrived at my friend's farm house. His wife met us and gave us the most unfriendly welcome that anyone could give by screaming at her husband for just leaving without her permission. She told him how the big black cow had practic-

137

ally broken her leg as she tried to milk her. She had a nasty black and blue bruise on the side of her right leg.

I didn't think she needed any of us, and felt terribly guilty for I had told my family what a wonderful crowd of people they were going to meet when they arrived there.

Chapter Ten
An Unchanging God

We phoned and asked many of our friends if they knew of any house that we could possibly rent. Our farmer friends advised us that there was no empty house for "miles around." I was very disappointed, and decided to go see the lady who worked in the Post Office because I felt that "she knew everything."

As I was about to enter the Post Office I looked down the road and saw a large U-haul truck standing in the driveway of a house. The people were taking furniture out of the house and loading it into the truck. That meant one thing: empty house.

I cancelled my visitation to the lady "that knew everything" and walked to the house where they were loading the furniture. I spoke to the man who once occupied the place, he said that the owner wanted to sell.

I told my wife. We both knew that we were in no position to buy a house, but I suggested that we ask our farmer friends to buy the house and then to rent it to us. We immediately bundled the girls into the car and drove to our farmer friends. I explained the circumstances and they regretted that they were unable to help us. The man said that they were so heavily mortgaged with the farm, the machinery and the buildings that it was impossible for them to get a further loan. He said that he knew without the shadow of a doubt that the Finance Corporation would "throw him out" if he asked for another loan.

My wife said very softly, "There would be no harm in trying, all they could do is throw you out." We all laughed but the farmer became serious and said to his wife, "Honey, why don't you go and see how much they want for the house, and then go to the Finance Company and see if they will lend you the money to buy the house. Then we will let the Rubenstein's rent the house from us."

For a moment there was no unity, and they argued back and forth which one should go. In a way this was most embarrassing, but I remembered "beggars can't be choosers." The lady left very annoyed, and my wife and I sat there very discouraged.

Two and a half hours later she came in half laughing, half crying, half dancing and half shouting, and in her hand she was twirling a key that was tied to a piece of twine. "It's ours, IT'S OURS," and rushed to her husband, wrapped her arms around him, kissed him on both cheeks and said, "Honey, I don't understand it but the manager of the Finance Company was only too pleased to give us the money to buy the house, and the owner was only too pleased to hand me the key."

I looked up toward heaven and tears ran down my face. I said aloud, "Jesus never fails." The following morning I made an emergency long distance telephone call to Toledo. I explained to our friends what had happened and that the empty house was waiting to be filled. George and Marie Miller had told us that God had instructed them to fully furnish a house for us when we had one to be furnished.

The Millers seemed to be happier than we were when we arrived there. They had gone to much trouble in cutting out furniture advertisements from the newspaper, and they had also written a long list of department stores that had furniture. I gazed at the list of furniture stores. I liked the name of one of the stores: Sears, Roebuck and Company. I said, "We would like to go to this place."

I recalled the psalmist David saying, "Once I was young, but now I am old. But I have never seen the righteous forsaken, nor His seed begging bread." I pushed my chest out as I realized that I was not a beggar but a member of royalty.

The day that the big Sears truck arrived to unload the furniture that George and Marie Miller of Toledo bought us was a big red-letter day in the lives of the Rubenstein family.

We placed the two older girls in school and were now "ready for big business for a big God."

When I was not in services I would help my farm friend. I enjoyed driving the tractor while Merle would stack bales of hay on the wagon behind. I had never believed in my wildest dreams that I would ever be driving a tractor.

Most of the people in that area were members of Mennonite churches, and were some of the most beautiful and precious people we had ever met. One of them, Dennis Nofziger, was most interested in my ministry. We would visit them often, and Dennis would invariably talk about the gift of healing. For hours we would discuss the healing ministry.

One morning Dennis went to the piggery and noticed one of his big sows lying motionless in the mud. He examined the animal and discovered that it was sickly. As he squatted there he thought about the things we had talked about. He looked around to see if anybody was watching him, and then laid his hands on the sow and asked the healer, Jesus of Nazareth, to heal the sow. Dennis nearly fell in the mud alongside the big pig as it jumped to its feet and ran away snorting, snorting, snorting. Later he said he was sure that the snorting sounded like "Hallelujah, hallelujah, hallelujah."

After several revival meetings I returned home and paid my farmer friend another visit. That evening I found my friend Dennis and his wife in close conversation with my wife. After a while Dennis began complaining that he was finding it difficult to get a man to help him with the door-hanging business. He had a franchise for a large area to hang doors. The doors were folding doors in service stations, and in private garages that could be operated either manually or electrically. There was so much carpentry work involved with it that he felt troubled that he could not keep his promises to his customers.

When he mentioned the word *carpentry* I became very interested. Before leaving they asked me to please make it a matter of prayer. I phoned Dennis a bit later and said: "There will be a man at your place to help you with the carpentry work tomorrow morning." Dennis became very excited and asked whether I was prophesying or whether I had contacted somebody. I told him, "Wait and see."

Very early the following morning I put on every warm piece of clothing I could find and drove through the snow and ice to the workshop on the farm. I could see a light in the kitchen and had scarcely turned off the engine when

141

Dennis hurried to meet me.

"Where is that guy that you promised would be here to help me?" he inquired.

"This is the guy standing right in front of you, Dennis."

He began to give me many reasons why he could not use me, and mentioned the fact that I was a preacher and not a carpenter.

When I told him about a very good friend of mine that was also a preacher and a carpenter 2,000 years ago, he got the message and put me to work.

I loved the work and that evening when he returned and examined what I had completed to be installed, he assured me that he had never come across a more reliable and polished carpenter. He handed me a check for $75. (I compared it with the same amount that I was receiving for one week's work in some of the churches.) My wife was also happy when I handed her the check. "Will this be your daily salary?" she asked very excitedly. I told her that the check was unexpected, but that I did not think that it would be a daily event, although I would not have complained if it were.

One evening as I was ready to leave the workshop, Dennis climbed into the car next to me and made me a most entertaining offer. He also explained that if I would join him and help him in his business, a great business could be developed. The offer he made me was most entertaining and moved my "Jewish heart."

I rushed home that evening and told my wife about the wonderful offer that Dennis had made. Before she could reply, I hastily continued to tell her how much more we would be earning in comparison to what I was earning "running from church to church."

My wife stared at me and smiled, nodding her head from side to side, and then said, "Hymie, why don't you go into the bathroom and wash your head."

I got the message, went to the bathroom, washed my head and came out and apologized to my wife for being so foolish to even consider swapping "the Bread of Life" for the door-hanging business.

During a revival in Indiana I received a telephone call from a man and his wife in Detroit, Michigan. They said they had a brand new Barracuda car that they wished to give me as a gift. I told them I was very busy in revival and that there was no time for fun and games. They insisted that the car was there if I wanted it.

I spoke to the pastor about the phone call. She suggested I go and fetch the car. She said she was sure the congregation would excuse me if I left.

I traveled to Detroit and called on Bill and Ann Kirkpatrick. They showed me a brand-new Barracuda car. It was a lovely cream color with beautiful red seats inside, and the gear lever down on the floor. As Bill handed me the keys he said, "Have a good time, Brother." We arranged that they would try and sell my Chevy station wagon, and I rode away in the beautiful free gift.

I pulled up at a cycle shop to ease my conscience and bought our youngest girl a beautiful cream-colored bicycle with red handle grips to match her daddy's car.

When I arrived home there was great excitement about the car, and when I took the bicycle out of the luggage box and handed it to my youngest daughter the excitement was even greater.

Later that evening I noticed my eldest girl standing on the patio, crying. I approached her with, "What's the trouble?"

She had just received her driver's license and wanted to borrow my car to attend a class meeting in her school that night. "Mama has forbidden me to ask you for the car," she cried.

I explained that the car had been given me "to be used for the work of the Lord."

She pointed to the school which was five blocks away and said, "But Daddy, you can see the school from here and the roads are wide, and there is no traffic, and you can watch me as I drive to school."

I walked inside the house and told my wife I did not see any danger in allowing the girl to drive to the school.

I called Leilah into the house, giving her good instructions. "Honey, I trust you, but all I ask you to do is to drive to school, and after your meeting I want you to drive directly home. In no way do I want you to pick up any of your school friends and allow them in the car with you."

She promised and hugged and kissed me, and took the keys to the car. I watched her as she slowly drove away to school.

The two girls and my wife and I watched a bit of television, then the girls retired and my wife and I sat in the living room talking. About twenty minutes to nine I told my wife I felt a strong call to go into the bedroom and pray.

I fell on my knees and said, "Dear Jesus, I do not know why I feel this sudden urge to consult you but here I am to tell you, dear Lord, that I appreciate you with every fiber in my body." I praised the Lord for about fifteen minutes and felt the urge leave me, and I returned to sit alongside my wife.

There was a loud knock on the door, and as I opened the door there were five or six young boys standing at the door overly excited. I knew they had bad news so I closed the door so that my wife could not hear what they were bursting to tell.

"Leilah has totally wrecked your car, and we think she is dead."

The door opened and my wife stood in the doorway. I went to her, and as gently as possible told her that Leilah had been in an accident, that she should not worry and wait for me to return.

We all hastened into their car and sped away to the scene of the wreck.

My heart sank to my feet as I saw what was once a beautiful cream-colored new Barracuda hanging from a large hook from a crane that the Auto Wrecking Company used. Lights of all colors were flickering, most of them from cops' cars that had arrived.

I jumped out of the car and rushed to the ambulance I saw on the side of the road. I got inside and found my daughter stretched out on the bed. My heart had fallen into my feet and now returned to its proper place as I noticed my daughter both breathing well, and also weeping.

"Daddy," she cried, "I'm terribly sorry that I wrecked your new car."

"Honey," I said, with a happy heart that my child was alive, "I can get a thousand new cars but I could never get another beautiful, lovely girl like you again."

As it turned out, my daughter was on her way back home after the class meeting and two of her friends, a young girl and boy had stopped her on the road and asked her to "Please take us home quickly." My daughter replied, "My father will kill me if I allow anybody in the car."

"Don't be chicken," they told her, "he will never know in a million years what you have done."

The challenge was more than she could bear so she allowed them into the car. The young boy sat in the back and the girl in the front. As she drove along the blacktop road the boy suggested a quicker way and instructed her to make a left turn onto a gravel road. On the gravel road they told her to see "what guts this thing has."

As the needle of the speedometer was hugging the 90-mph mark a car suddenly backed out of a driveway right into the path of the oncoming Barracuda car. My daughter instinctively pushed on the brake pedal and the car careened into the left side ditch. This caused the car to somersault, and as the nose hit the ground, the windshield went out and my daughter went out through the windshield. The car crossed the road again and went into the ditch on the other side and once again made another somersault, landing on the back, forcing the boy in the back out of the large back window. The girl in the front was locked tightly under the front seat. After the officers had managed to get the girl out of the car and examined her, there was nothing wrong with her apart from a small mark on her left knee. The boy was taken to the hospital where he received fourteen stitches to close a gash in his back.

All the parents were thankful that nothing more tragic had taken place.

We received a visit from a man with the insurance company and he informed us that the car was a total wreck. He also said that we could decide between two factors. "You can either go and find yourself another car, or we will give you a check immediately for $1,750." Without hesitation my wife said, "Money." The poor man had scarcely finished signing the check when my wife relieved him of it.

That evening, Mrs. Hegle who had been healed of emphysema in the service in Defiance, Ohio, paid us a visit. She had heard of our misfortune and told me that she had an old model Ford car that she was willing to give me.

The following day we had the license transferred into my name. I was also informed that the Chevrolet station wagon had been sold, so we were now free of debt as far as cars were concerned.

Chapter Eleven
Little Is Much
When God Is in It

Church revivals became routine. At times I believed that the churches were praying: "Father, you keep him humble and we will keep him poor." I decided I could do better and began arranging my own campaigns.

I contacted a Holland couple who now lived in California. I had originally met them in South Africa. Rita and Simon VanDrimmilen were two of the greatest singers that many people, including myself, had openly stated that we had ever heard. I invited them to join me in a campaign that I had arranged in the Elks Temple in downtown Detroit.

I promised to pay necessary expenses and then called on the caretaker of the Elks Temple. I told him that I had hired the Temple "by faith." He assured me that it was unlikely that I could get the hall at such short notice. He also informed me that an evangelist from Texas had just concluded a campaign. I asked him about the cost of hiring the hall. He said the Texas evangelist had paid $150 a night. When he mentioned the amount, my heart missed a beat.

"Sir," I said, "I cannot afford that amount of money myself, and would like you to please listen to my testimony and then consider the price you would ask."

I quickly gave him my testimony and noticed tears in his eyes as he said, "Mr. Rubenstein, I am only the caretaker here, but I will speak to the committee and see whether they can give you the hall any cheaper than what they had given it to the other man." If I would phone him the following day he would let me know.

"How much are you prepared to pay for the hall, Mr. Rubenstein?" he asked.

"Ten dollars a night, Sir." I noticed he nearly choked on either chewing gum or tobacco. He looked at me and I could see by the look on his face that he thought that I was crazy.

I slapped him on the back and said, "God bless you real good, friend."

I did not phone him the following morning but called on him personally. I was happy to see that he was happy when I arrived. He unlocked a small partition that had the sign "Strictly Private," and had me sit in a chair. Before I could ask him any questions he said, "The committee refuses to accept your offer of $10 a night." He looked at my reactions and I knew that all he could see in my face was great disappointment. "Do you know what they expect from you, Mr. Rubenstein?" he asked raising his voice, giving me the impression that they would expect me to pay what the Texas evangelist had been paying. I sat there and nodded my head at him, and then I waited.

"Twelve dollars a night!" he shouted as he jumped into the air and rushed toward me. I jumped into the air with him and rushed to embrace him, and together we stood there laughing heartily.

For one week we had the most wonderful campaign. Many church members attended and far outnumbered the unbelievers that had wandered in. The thing that pleased me mostly was that I personally had control of the plentiful finances.

I decided to use a new method for offerings and placed a large garbage container in front of the pulpit and compelled the audience to "bring your offerings" according to the scriptures. They seemed to enjoy it thoroughly, but when I found that I had taken $1,000 the first week I knew, or I *thought* that my heavenly Father was happy.

I was in the basement of the home that I was staying in having a long talk with "my director." He spoke to my heart and seemed to ask me whether it was more important for me to "work for money," or "to work for Me?"

I wept and repented that I had done the thing that was an abomination in His sight. I had made "filthy lucre" the most important thing in my ministry.

I explained to the VanDrimmilens that I was going to stop the services that we were in, and that I intended returning to churches where I could edify pastors, elders, deacons and congregations. This I continued to do and I knew that

God was happy up there in heaven, and that all was right with the world . . . regarding me and finances.

A most charming gentleman approached me one day and introduced himself as Pastor John Stevens. He asked if I would hold a series of meetings in his church. He took me to the church and I found he had converted a small storefront into a church. I would have preferred to have ministered in a larger place, but I had become most cautious about my preferences after the Elks Temple episode.

The first week's nightly meetings were wonderfully blessed, and the wonderful God that we were advertising became more wonderful as we carried on. One night the pastor told me he had received a telephone call from a lady who said she did not believe as I believed and was not prepared to sit in on one of my meetings. But she asked whether the pastor thought I would pray for her before the meeting. I paid little attention to this as I thought it rather stupid.

As usual, the service began with praises and singing, and the orchestra was "very fired up." One of the ladies sitting on a chair alongside the middle aisle jumped up from the chair and began dancing in the aisle. The pastor and I laughed as we enjoyed watching the lady spinning like a top up and down the aisle. The orchestra stopped and the dancer stopped and returned to her seat.

As I stood at the pulpit ready to deliver the message that God had laid upon my heart I said, "Before I begin my message we have received a telephone call from a lady who has asked that I pray for her before my message so that she might leave as she has more important things to do, or she thinks that she has more important things to do," I added. "Would the lady, if she is present, kindly come to the front?"

To my surprise, and to the surprise of Brother Stevens, the lady who walked to the front was the lady who had been spinning like a top in the aisle.

She stood close to the platform, and as I stood before her I felt in my heart that there was absolutely nothing wrong with her physically, and told her so. She clapped her hands excitedly and said, "You had better believe it, man. Whatever was troubling me for the last few months left me as I was dancing in the aisle."

That testimony of the unbeliever thrilled us that night, and it glorified the Saviour, the One who was "no respecter of persons."

Later that year I was called to minister to a Methodist Community Church in downtown Detroit. A lovelier group of people I had not met. They made me so very welcome and did all they could to advertise the meetings. This was the first time I was holding a series of meetings for the Methodist denomination, but I knew that it would be well blessed. One of the things that was most difficult for me to get used to was the fact that the entire meeting was controlled by *numbers* and by *time*. Each night there were numbers on the wall indicating what songs would be sung out of the hymnal. I was also instructed not to speak longer than thirty minutes. I pleaded with the minister to give me an additional ten minutes if possible. At first he was reluctant and then agreed.

After one evening service a lady came to the front holding a very small boy by the hand. She said he was a victim of terrible migraine headaches. Automatically I moved to lay my hands upon him, but she cautioned me saying, "We don't do that here."

I realized where I was, and she suggested that we go into the prayer room where I could secretly pray for the boy, and I agreed. I did not notice that a few other women had joined in our march to the prayer room before I could close the door. I spoke a while to them and then walked over to the young boy, laid my hands on him and asked the "migraine-healing God" to heal him."

As I was praying I felt the presence of "the Holy One," and knew that there was a "power present to heal." I had no intentions of allowing that power to be wasted so I laid my hands on the ladies that were there praying with me, and they were all baptized with the Holy Ghost and received "the gift of tongues."

After a Texas meeting I drove to Louisiana. I had been told about Pastor Mildred Greene who was pastoring an Assembly of God church in Bossier City. I had seen photographs of her, so that when she walked past my car with her two friends I recognized her immediately. I climbed out of the car and said, "Pastor Greene." She stopped, and I knew that I had not made a mistake. I introduced myself to her and asked about the possibility of having a revival in her church.

We worked out a schedule for me to have a week's services in her church. We phoned anyone that we thought could be helpful and would be interested. I started the first night with only a handful of people, and I felt that I could hear an abundance of rain approaching. We had switched off the electricity in the church, and were just in the throes of locking the doors when a car pulled up outside the church.

A couple that I recognized had been in the meeting got out of the car. They were both very excited and were crying and told the pastor that on their way home God had spoken to both of them and instructed them to "Go back immediately to the church and give your hearts to Jesus."

We unlocked the door, turned on the lights, went to the altar and were thrilled to lead this couple out of the worldly darkness into God's wonderful light. I knew if a series of meetings started off the way this one had that the end would be far, far better than the beginning.

I recalled the time that Jesus spoke at the marriage in Cana and turned the water into wine when the ruler of the feast said, "Every man at the beginning doth set forth the good wine but thou hast kept the good wine until the last."

The attendance began to improve from night to night and after the first week we decided to run the second week. A fine orchestra had sprung up from nowhere and we decided to hold one or two open-air services around the shopping areas.

The church bus had large placards advertising the meetings. On a given day many gathered at a shopping center to advertise "Victory in Jesus." A truck was standing alongside the bus with the church orchestra on it. The music attracted hundreds of people and the singing was beautiful.

After a while I climbed onto the truck, and opened my Bible and began to talk about the victorious life that God's children could enjoy from day to day. We extended an invitation to the church and that night we found quite a few who had accepted the invitation. The church was now three-fourths full and that consisted of 200 people.

I was staying in the Captain Shreve Hotel and, as was customary, I was doing my early morning prayer exercise when I felt impressed to arrange an interview with the mayor of Shreveport. I had heard that there had been much trouble and civil rights demonstrations. I knew a solution to the problem and wanted to make my Friend who was the solution known to the city.

I was advised by the lady who sat at a desk in the foyer of the city hall that the mayor was not due back until the following day. "But you can see the sheriff if you please," she offered.

I readily accepted the offer and was ushered into the office of the sheriff. I spoke about how I enjoyed my stay in his lovely city. I could see that he was fascinated with my strange accent. I told him what Jesus had done for me and that Jesus could do the same for him. He sat and ate the Bread of Life as I served it. I concluded and thanked him for listening. He immediately called the receptionist and told her to book me "definitely tomorrow at 10 to see the mayor." I thanked him heartily for his interest and left.

The following morning at twenty minutes before 10 I spoke to the receptionist. She remarked that I was "rather on the early side." I said, "Better early than not at all." We laughed, and she referred to the trouble that seemed to be brewing in the city.

At 10 she opened the door and signaled for me to see the mayor. He received me as though I was a lost friend, and said the sheriff had already given him my testimony and said that he was "so thankful unto the good Lord for going what He had for me."

I talked about the trouble that was in the city. He said, "I'm sure that God will work out a way." I readily agreed and answered, "If we will allow Him to, I am sure that He would only be too pleased to."

The mayor said he wished that he could help me in some way. He seemed surprised when I told him that I was interested in holding a few nights' services in the convention hall in the city, "but I cannot afford it."

"I would like the people of Shreveport to hear your testimony, and I will do my best to see that you get the chance to tell as many as possible what Almighty God has done for you. I will phone the caretaker of the Convention Hall and arrange with him about getting the loan of the hall for a week," he said.

I shook his hand hard and long and prayed with the mayor of Shreveport and left, and went directly to the Convention Hall to find the caretaker. I introduced myself and told him that I intended using one of the halls in the convention center for religious services. He explained that he had just decided to take his annual vacation and go to Florida, that business had been bad and that the halls had not been rented for some time, but that he would be prepared to cancel his vacation for another week and I could have one of the halls.

I reported that I had spoken to the mayor, and if he would phone him he would know what to do. As he was speaking to the mayor I could see a smile on his face as he told him that he had somebody who wanted to rent the hall "D" for a week's religious services. He asked, "Sir, what should we charge him?" He put down the receiver and when he approached me the look on his face reminded me of somebody that had been chewing chalk. I got the Convention Hall, "No Charge."

When I got back to the hotel I phoned Pastor Greene and the other members, and once again we all got very busy phoning as many as we could inviting them to "Hall D" in the Shreveport Convention Building.

After each meeting the caretaker would complain that the meetings were running too long. He stated that he did not intend staying longer than 10 any evening. This was a drawback but we gave it to "the One who could make mighty changes."

The fourth night He made a mighty change.

The mighty change took part in the life of the caretaker. When I asked for the show of hands of people who wanted to receive Christ of Calvary as their personal Saviour, standing at the back of the hall with his hands high in the air, weeping unashamedly and loudly, stood the caretaker.

As the people were leaving the place I walked up to the man and said, "Sir, I hope we are not late again tonight."

He put his arm around me and said, "Preacher man, you can run as long as you like any night and every night." We did finish with a mighty blessing from God.

I enjoyed driving my old Chevy car back through the different states into Michigan to have one more revival in the church of Rev. Takett before returning home to Ohio. I was sorry when the revival came to a close but I did feel that it was time, after four months, to return home to my wife and three lovely girls.

Upon my return home there was a special invitation waiting for me to speak in the First Baptist Church of Defiance. I phoned Rev. Russell Bowditch and told him it would be a pleasure for me to speak in his church the following Sunday.

That Sunday morning we each dressed extra smartly as this was the first time I would be speaking in a Baptist church. I did hope to make an impression there. With the help of God I knew that I could not possibly fail.

We arrived and were all accepted by everyone in the church. Such Christian love could not be found in every Christian church as we found there. I was escorted to the pastor's office who seemed surprised to see me. He explained that he had intended for me to speak that evening because it was Mother's Day and he had prepared a message for the morning. I told him it was more than a pleasure for me to listen to him.

Pastor Bowditch then approached the pulpit and explained to the people that he had invited me to speak that evening and extended an invitation to everyone to be at the service that night. "Nevertheless friends, I would like Rev. Rubenstein to just say a few words this morning so that we can get some idea of what we can expect this evening."

I stepped to the pulpit and once again knew that my Friend Jesus had stepped alongside me. I spoke for a short time and the windows of heaven were suddenly opened and God poured out a deluge of blessings in the place. Pastor Bowditch jumped to his feet and signalled me to continue. After I had completed with what I felt I had to say I handed the service to the pastor. He stood at the pulpit weeping. I was weeping too. He explained that for the past six years he had desired "so much to give an altar call" but had failed to do so. "I do not intend failing this morning," he stated.

"If there is anyone here who would like me, their pastor, to pray for them this morning would you kindly come forward." He stepped off the platform and stood with his arms outstretched toward the congregation.

It was quite obvious from the reaction that he received that the people were not used to altar calls. Many came forward and began embracing the pastor and holding his extended arms, while others that could not reach him embraced the others about him. In between cries of joy the pastor thanked God that the barrier that had stood between him and his flock had been broken down. I had never before seen a total congregation cry together but that morning on Mother's Day, as the pastor and I stood in the doorway to greet each person as they left, there was not one dry eye.

In a meeting in New York I was speaking to approximately 150 people who desired "the baptism in the Holy Ghost with the evidence of speaking with other tongues."

I told them how I had received this experience and that they had probably heard of many others receiving this experience in many other ways. I told them of a time that I had been preaching a message, "Power For This Hour" and had become so enveloped in the message that I jumped off the platform and grabbed the front row of benches to steady myself. Unfortunately the benches had not been secured to the floor so I fell over them and grabbed the second row of benches hoping to be supported. The second row proved to be no different, so I fell over those also and lay under the third row. I stood to my feet and tried to get myself straightened up knowing that my behavior was not appreciated by everyone, but I thanked God for the Christians there with a sense of humor.

I closed the service and a few months later I went back to the same church where the first one to greet me upon my arrival was a middle-aged woman. She warmly shook my hand and welcomed me and laughingly said, "Brother Hymie, do you remember the last time you were here?"

I assured her that never in my life would I ever forget it. She answered, "Do you know Brother, that when you fell under the third row of benches God baptized me with the Holy Ghost in the back of the church?"

As I told this story to people in the Americana Hotel in New York I told them that I did not intend falling over any benches, but that God had indicated a much easier way to receive power from on high. I referred the group to the book of Luke, chapter 11 and verse 13. I had only begun to read the verse and had quoted the first six words, "If ye then, being evil, know" and right then God baptized the 42 people that occupied the front rows of seats. I stood there amazed and my Norwegian Brother Simon Vikse stood alongside me just as amazed as I. I realized more than ever "that God was God and by no means bound to the ideas and thoughts of man."

Chapter Twelve

The Nazarene Keeps Piloting, Watching, Waiting

A young boy got saved in my tabernacle one Sunday morning. The following Sunday morning he made it his business to sit on the seat in the front row.

As I watched him I could see the anxiety, and I could feel the fire burning in his bones. I knew he wanted to tell the world what had happened to him the previous Sunday when he presented his life to the Lord Jesus Christ.

I moved to the pulpit. "Is there anyone here who would like to encourage us by giving us a short firey testimony?" I knew in my heart that that was exactly what the new convert was waiting for.

In his excitement to give his testimony the Bible fell out of his hands, and as he leaned over to pick up the Bible his spectacles fell off his face. As he was trying to retrieve both the Bible and the spectacles some pencils fell out of his pocket. I felt sorry for the young man but continued with the service.

The following Sunday morning the young man was there again, and I knew without fail this time he was going to tell it with a greater zeal than the Sunday before because he had had yet another week "to get charged up."

I walked to the pulpit and said, "Friends, I wonder if there is anyone here this morning who would like to give us a short firey testimony of what the Lord Jesus Christ means to them and what He has done for them?" I thought it would be an automatic response from the young man, but others kept jumping up and testifying. I then looked at the young man but he was sneezing and coughing and trying to control the tears that were coming out of his eyes. I felt I could not allow this to hinder the service, so I asked for the choir to sing.

As the choir was singing the young man ceased his

coughing and sneezing spell, took his Bible and walked out of the church. I could see he was terribly upset, discouraged and disappointed.

He walked down the road for two blocks where he sat on a bench in the park. As he sat there the Lord spoke to his heart and said, "My son, be not afraid and neither be dismayed, the church is not the only place that you can testify. Testify right here in the park and tell these people what wonderful and great things I have done for you."

The young man stood to his feet and then stood on the bench and began to tell what he had been instructed to tell. For thirty minutes he explained about the peace of mind he had now experienced and so many other things that had taken place in his life over the past two weeks since he had decided to "make Jesus his pilot" and hand his life completely over to Him.

"This took place in the church down the road here two weeks ago," he told the people. At the conclusion he decided to sit on the bench.

"Once again he heard a voice say, "Give an altar call." For a moment the young man did not know what to do as he was not a pastor, neither was he an elder, neither was he a deacon, but the word "call" could only mean one thing. So he called those who had heard him and were desirous of having the same experience that he had had to come to him and allow him to pray for them and introduce them to "that wonderful giver of eternal life."

Much to the young man's surprise 36 people came and kneeled down on the green grass and looked up into the blue sky and gave their hearts to the Lamb of God, the king of glory.

The following Sunday morning I noticed the young man once again on the front row in the same seat. This time I hoped he would be able to give his testimony. I had scarcely asked for testimonies when he was already standing on his feet and said, "Devil, if you trip me up again this morning, I'll take you down to the park and win 36 souls for Jesus."

I was to speak in the Assembly of God church in Midland, Michigan, when I received a phone call from a young

158

lady. As she spoke she wept and said she had heard my testimony while in Detroit and did not believe it. She said she was phoning from a rest area on Highway 75 and was going to commit suicide.

I spoke to her a long time and told her how futile it was to do a thing like that. She screamed at me, rebuked me and commanded me not to interfere in her life.

I asked her to do herself and myself and God a special favor by coming to the church in Midland and allowing me to speak with her. She flatly refused and slammed down the receiver.

I walked into the church and fell on my knees at the altar and cried to God to help her.

I knew my prayers had once again been answered for an hour later I saw a young lady drive into the driveway of the church in one of the smartest, brightest, shiniest Mustang cars. She had had that thing fitted with mirrors wherever a mirror could be fitted. She had had that thing fitted with racing stripes wherever a racing stripe could be fitted.

I walked out of the church, opened the door and climbed into the car next to her and knew immediately who she was.

As I was counseling her I looked down on the floorboard; I saw it was covered with blood.

"What on earth have you done, young lady?" I asked her. I grabbed both hands and could see that she had cut her wrists badly.

I rushed her into the church and bandaged the wrists. She kneeled down at the altar with me and raised those hands to Christ Jesus, repented and once again God's tender mercy and amazing grace took her back into the fold.

The young lady promised she would now go and have those wounds attended to, and until today she still raises her wrist-scarred arms to the Lamb of God who wrapped His arms around her that afternoon in a church in Midland, Michigan, and said to her, "You are my child."

As I have traveled around the world I have met thousands who have been possessed with a suicidal spirit.

There was a time that approximately 16,000 people in the United States of America were committing suicide while

50,000 were being killed on the highways. Today that figure has gone even higher, many of those highway deaths are suicidal.

I was asked to testify in a camp meeting held by the Pentecostal Church of God in Michigan. There was a large crowd and wall-to-wall people—many glorifying and magnifying the Christ of Nazareth.

After I testified I left the hall and was stopped by a young lady outside the door who began weeping and trembling. I waited for some time for her to calm herself and then she said, "Sir, if you had not come and given your testimony I would have been dead tonight."

She pointed to a tree that stood nearby next to a corrugated building and explained she had hidden some rope under her bed and intended climbing on the roof of the building and tying the rope to a limb that extended close to the roof of the building and jumping off the roof. She wrapped her arms around me and said most humbly, "Thank you, kind sir."

I began to wonder how many others were participating in that campground convention who were dissatisfied, defeated and sick and tired of being sick and tired.

I wondered how many millions who had been labeled "Christians" were hungry and thirsty for the Bread of Life and the Living Water, and because of not being fed had become destitute.

I wondered how many millions of good "church members" were contemplating "putting an end to it all" because all they had been hearing was politics, watergate, Vietnam, communism, Ouija boards, and many unnecessary doctrines. Many have complained to me that the pulpit in their church was being used as a worldly media instead of a godly media. Jesus said: "Feed my sheep," and the Word of God was given to edification, and edification only.

A young boy was chasing his elder brother around the house when suddenly his brother slammed the door in his face. Strangely enough the young boy's tongue was caught in the door.

160

The mother phoned me and was frantic and asked me to please come immediately.

When I arrived I was ushered into the bathroom where the boy was bleeding profusely. His tongue was hanging by a very thin piece of skin on the side.

The mother who was now in deep shock was explaining to me that she had been trusting God to stop the bleeding and to heal what was once a tongue. She asked me to join her in prayer, but I grabbed the nearest towel, wrapped it around the boy's face and rushed him to the nearby hospital.

The mother and other believers did not appreciate the action I had taken, but I believed that God did, and felt that He had given me both common sense and a sound mind.

As the doctor began stitching the tongue together I waited outside the emergency theater unable to watch the operation. The boy cried and pushed the doctor's hand away and by the signs that he made they understood that he wanted me back in the room. The nurse came and explained that the boy wanted me to be with him.

This was not the best of news of the day for me, but I walked in and stood alongside the boy so he could see me, but I did not look at him. He mumbled and grumbled to catch my attention to make sure that I was looking at him while the doctor was sewing his tongue together. To make the boy very happy and myself most unhappy, I stood there watching the operation.

When the doctor said, "It is finished, his tongue will grow together again," one of the biggest sighs of relief that I ever sighed, I sighed right there as the boy closed his mouth and we left for home.

Many believers challenged me for taking the boy to the hospital.

One man who had spoken at one of my meetings condemned the medical profession and said that it was a disgrace for a believer "to depend on the arm of flesh, with the arms of God always present to heal."

A few days later my wife had a vision about that man and saw that one of his feet was thickly bandaged. She was not usually given to visions, but I advised her to phone that man and tell him what she had seen.

The man was glad she phoned and told her what she had seen had come to pass. "I am laid up in bed with gout in both my feet. I have had three of the best specialists come to visit me and unless they are able to help me I don't think I'll ever be able to walk again."

It is easy for the people who are well and strong to denounce the medical profession, but I found that when those same people got sick and physically affected, they were the first to call for medical aid.

I have found many Christians who could believe while things were going well and in their favor, but should any ill wind or boisterous wave give them an unexpected jar, both their belief and faith were easily shattered.

I have noticed some of the professing spiritual giants who constantly "ate from the tree of knowledge" were very strong in the head, but very weak in the heart.

In London a lady explained to an audience about the mighty miracle that God had performed in her life. "He healed and filled four teeth in my mouth," she said.

I knew it was possible for God to do all things, but this was one story that I had heard many times that I desired to have first-hand evidence on. The lady told many people the story, but I could feel that she tried to avoid me.

One day I could see her slowly join me in the seat I was sitting in in the foyer and said, "You know, brother, I have told practically everybody in the hotel about the way God has filled my teeth, but you."

I asked her why that was, and she said she did not know. She then proceeded to tell me how God had filled two upper and two lower teeth.

In my spirit I felt like a doubting Thomas, but I really wanted to believe what she was telling me in such an excited way. "May I look at these teeth, please?" I asked.

She replied, "They are there all right, two on the top and two on the bottom on the right-hand side of my mouth." She did her best to assure me, trusting that I would readily accept, as so many others had readily accepted her story.

I bent forward and said, "Push back your head and open your mouth and let me see."

She hesitated and then obliged by half opening her

mouth. I said, "Come on now lady, get that big mouth of yours open, I want to see the work that you have told me God has done in that mouth of yours."

She opened her mouth wide and I looked inside. Sure enough there were two teeth at the back and two teeth on the bottom that had been filled. I put my finger in her mouth and felt the fillings. I removed my finger and she closed her mouth and I said, "Lady, were those black fillings put in there by God?" I looked at her, defying her to tell me anything but the truth.

She hesitated and looked away for a moment, and I knew right there that she had lied to me, and many others.

"Well, to tell the truth," she said very slowly, "the black fillings that you see in these four teeth were put in there by a dentist, but one day I had such terrible pain in those four teeth that I went to a service and asked for prayer and God healed me and took away the pain."

People have said to me, "A man prayed for me and healed my heart."

I asked the same people whether they had ever had heart trouble, and they replied, "No, but the man who prayed for me told me that I did and he healed me."

Others have told me how they had been baptized with the Holy Ghost and received the gift of tongues by muttering the same words as the preacher had told them to mutter. "Hymie, this is my tongue, listen to it," they would tell me. And like a parrot they would say words that they had been saying for weeks and months and years.

My heart often nearly breaks when I see psychology being used by many speakers. I know full well people do not need psychology because many of the psychiatrists are in worse shape than their clients.

What everyone needs is not love but Jesus, who would not only give love, but peace, joy, goodness, gentleness, meekness, faith, temperance and mercy.

Chapter Thirteen

Be Strong in the Lord Always

At times I would contact the lazy preacher who would spend most of his time "waiting upon the leading of the Lord" simply because he had not prepared a message to feed the flock. Others would find it easier to speak about a "body ministry" so that practically everybody could take over the service, which prevented them from doing any praying or studying a message beforehand. This I knew was the main course for God's sheep to continue being hungry and thirsty for the food and for the water that only the Lamb, the Christ of Calvary, could give to drought-stricken souls.

Three times Jesus told Peter, "Feed my lambs, feed my sheep, feed my sheep."

At times I would sit in on a Sunday school lesson and the person in charge would relate to something they had seen on the way to church. If it was not a wreck along the way it was a new building that had been built, and there would be a lengthy discussion about what the "model cities" and other businesses intended doing in the downtown area. One had heard this, another had heard that, and another believed this and another believed that and twenty-five minutes would be taken up by the class discussing the new improvements that were going to be made to the city. Suddenly the one in charge would look at the clock and say, "My word, there are only three minutes remaining before the first bell and we have done nothing about the lesson." The first bell would ring, the second bell would ring and the hungry sheep would remain hungry with only building programs in their minds and nothing in their souls.

I am persuaded that Paul the Apostle felt very strongly that apart from the gifts of the Spirit being in operation, and apart from the fruits of the Spirit being in operation, and apart from much prayer and much fasting, we most certainly "had to be strong in the Lord."

Some of the greatest spiritual giants that I have known flowing with knowledge had had a little Delilah approach them and because all their knowledge was head knowledge they were unable to overcome temptation that was placed their way. Like Samson, they had their hair cut away and fell. Like Peter, when a little girl challenged him the day that Pontius Pilate was interrogating Jesus.

One Full Gospel Businessmen's Fellowship chapter president said one evening, "Brother Hymie, we are so happy that you brought your wife along. It is so seldom that the speakers bring their wives along."

I thanked him for his kind remark and assured him that it was a precaution that I felt necessary to take so I wouldn't run off with somebody else's wife. We laughed at the remark but I think we both knew that as things were taking place among different married and unmarried parties it was not a joke. When I recall a pastor friend of mine who had built a most beautiful church, and how in a split second he was trapped by a Delilah, I knew that if it could happen to such a man of God as he, it was a warning to other men of God "to beware."

My pastor friend had mentioned that one of his young members had bought herself a new piano. He said that she had phoned him to come and play the piano to test the volume, sound, etc., because he was a famous pianist. He related how he had sat there playing the songs from the old-fashioned church hymnal and how that young lady had slipped onto the bench next to him and how they sat there singing. He praised her on the choice of her piano, and as he stood to leave she stood alongside the piano to make way for him to leave. Most unintentionally, he wrapped his arms around her, squeezed and kissed her and left suddenly realizing that in that split second he had committed an act that was an abomination in the sight of the God he was serving. He returned to his study and contemplated what he had done.

While he was contemplating the telephone rang and it was that young girl that he had embraced and kissed. He apologized for his actions and hoped that she would forgive him and not mention the incident to anybody.

The girl said there was no need to apologize but that she felt it was her duty to apologize to him. "My behavior was so unnecessary, pastor," she said to him so sweetly, so seemingly sincerely and delicately.

"Hymie, I did the worst thing I've ever done in my life. I went back to the home of that girl," he confessed to me.

The outcome was serious. The pastor was relieved of his pastorate, his membership card was taken from him, and he left both a pregnant wife and children to go to be with Delilah. Small wonder St. Paul said, "Finally brethren, be strong in the Lord."

A speaker that once went to Alabama holding services felt that it was in order to kiss every lady after he had prayed for them. If only he had understood that this is not in accordance with the will of God. When a pastor told me this and said that he had spoken to the man about it, the man had said, "That is just fringe benefits." The pastor said he could not have a man like that in his church because the man did not understand the things of God. Yet another preacher who went around the country serenading rich widows with his beautiful voice attempted to persuade them to leave money to him in their wills. I was a personal friend of one of these ladies, and told her that God Almighty had spoken concerning such men. "For of this sort are they which creep into houses and lead captive silly women laden with sins, led away with divers lusts."

One of the most distinguished preachers it had been my good fortune to meet joined me one night on my platform. He assured me that he would cancel all the services in his church in order for the congregation to attend my services. I was thrilled about it and asked him to make that announcement, and to take the service that night if he so desired.

The man thrilled me by his mannerisms and his charm.

He did not arrive as promised the next evening, neither did he arrive the next.

From some of the members who had come I was informed that he had been trapped by some of his congregation, and his wife found him seducing one of his members in her home. To me it was a great shock, but that denomination decided to move him out of that area into another area to continue his duties as a pastor.

In many cities I have visited, both with my wife or without, people have mentioned so casually that they were now living with their third or fourth wife, or with the third or fourth husband as though they were buying loaves of bread from the grocery store. A well-known friend of mine relieved his best friend of his wife, much to the disappointment of his best friend and of his own wife.

As we see these things taking place it is a warning to "hold fast that which is good, and to allow no man to take my crown."

One morning during my stay in the Hyatt Lodge in Pasadena, the young girl who cleaned my room daily, walked into the room and complained about the heat. As I stood behind a partition shaving, she came behind the partition and quickly pulled off the shirt she was wearing and stood there topless. I got a fright because this was the first time such a thing had happened to me.

She smiled and before I could make any remarks or wash the shaving cream off my face she pulled off the trousers she was wearing, and I don't remember ever a time in my life making the speedy exit in such good time as I did then.

The following day I was glad to see a new maid attending my room. She advised me that the old one had left.

"Be strong in the Lord and in the power of his might" is still good advice!

Such incidences remind me that there is a devil who walks around like a roaring lion seeing who he can destroy, and that I should be aware of the fact that he was after those that he did not already have.

In Oberlin, Ohio, I was asked to conduct a revival in the new church that had been built. The new church had been built because the pastor had been removed from his pulpit in another church because he had told the lesbians in the church that they were an abomination in the sight of God. Those that he had accused had called a special emergency meeting to move him out of the church in spite of their husbands entirely agreeing with what the pastor had said.

In San Francisco I was amazed to find that one of the most beautiful churches I had seen had a membership of homosexuals only. Also I have found churches, well-known in the country, that were holding special seminars called "seminars for gays."

I have studied the book of Romans in the first chapter where God had said how He had given some up to uncleanness through the lust of their hearts, to dishonor their own bodies between themselves, men with men and women with women. I knew that this was both an abomination in the sight of God and a stench in His nostrils. I spoke to one lesbian about this and she was on the verge of attacking me for what I had told her.

Invariably young men and young women come forward to be delivered of homosexuality. During my messages I have never mentioned the word, but under the moving of the Holy Ghost they have found themselves to be in a hopeless condition and on their way to hell.

It was small wonder that Jesus, after speaking to his disciples, opened their understanding that they might understand the scriptures. And if Jesus and the Holy Ghost and God himself do not open the understanding of these men, and including the apostle, the evangelist, the preacher, the teacher, and the missionary, how shall they ever be able to discern what the will of God is in these times?

A young couple in Jackson, Alabama, visited the Drive-in Cinema practically every night. There was a large sign along the road that had to be seen by everyone driving by. The large lettering on the sign read: "The blood of Jesus Christ cleanses from all sin." They had looked upon that sign possibly hundreds of times. At no time did they understand what it meant. One evening on their way to the cinema they both looked at the sign and God opened their understanding. The young man drove off the road, switched off the ignition and wept. Much to his surprise the young lady next to him was weeping too. He was about to explain to her what had taken place but she said that it was not necessary because she knew that the same thing that had taken place in his life had taken place in her life. They made a U-turn and returned to the city to find a pastor that could explain this happening in their lives. They discussed the sign: "The blood of Jesus Christ cleanses from all sin" Once again my heavenly Father proved to me that people would never be able to recognize Him except they walked and talked in the Spirit.

God spoke to my heart and said, "They that are after the flesh do mind the things of the flesh, and to be carnally minded is death. They that are in the flesh do not please God but they that are in the Spirit, the Spirit of God dwells in them. And if Christ be in us the body is dead because of sin, and the Spirit is life because of righteousness. And if the Spirit that raised Jesus from the dead dwell in you, you are alive, not dead. For as many as are led by the Spirit of God, they are the sons of God. The Spirit bears witness that we are the children of God."

My eyes were well opened and I am enjoying spiritual twenty-twenty vision, and seeing as the Spirit of Christ within me is seeing. God spoke again to my heart and said, "I will destroy the wisdom of the wise and will bring to nothing the understanding of the prudent. Has not God made foolish the wisdom of this world? For the world by wisdom knew not God, it pleased God by the foolishness of preaching to save them that believed and that God has chosen the foolish things of the world to confound the wise, and God has chosen the weak things of the world to confound the things that are mighty."

I felt like a man walking on cloud Number Nine realizing that so many were constantly eating "at the tree of knowledge" jamming and cramming their heads with "the letter of God" that killeth instead of "the Spirit of God" that giveth eternal, everlasting, permanent life. It is because of this a man in Texas would run away with his best friend's wife, and another preacher would run away with his organist and leave his wife.

My heart is distressed when I find that the so-called shepherds refuse to understand that a good position or a good home, or a good income, or a good credit card, is not the answer to a good ministry.

Many of the Jewish people understand the things that are important to God better than many Gentiles who profess that they do.

Many, many times I've been approached and asked, "Brother Hymie, how should we approach the Jewish people, or how should we work among the Jewish people?"

I have only one reply for them: Live the life of Jesus.

If ever there was a time that the Jewish people are looking for their Messiah, it is in these times. I have found them watching and looking for Him in those who have confessed that they have Him to no avail.

During a tent campaign one evening I noticed twelve Jewish business men walk in and seat themselves. I was happy to be able to help them to understand that the Jesus of Calvary was without any doubt "the King of the Jews."

By all intents and purposes it seemed as though that dozen Jewish men had really enjoyed the service. It also appeared that they were reluctant to go at the conclusion thereof. I introduced myself to them individually, and they complimented me on my "lecture."

The eldest man asked if I would accompany the group to his home. "We have a few things to discuss with you," he said.

As we sat in a beautiful, richly-furnished living room the eldest man said, "Mr. Rubenstein, as we entered your tent this evening there was a man standing in the entrance hall wearing a bright red jacket; is he one of your Christians?"

I recalled the man I had appointed to hand out the song sheets. I did not hesitate to tell the man that as far as I was concerned, "He is a Christian."

The man smiled and said, "Would you do me a favor by coming with me to my furniture store and examining my ledger with me, because I can assure you that this man has not paid me one penny in the last three and a half years for practically a household of furniture that he bought from me."

Naturally, this was a great surprise to me, for I had held that man in high esteem.

As best I could, I explained to the interrogators that I could not hold myself responsible for the actions of others, but could only tell them of my own opinions.

They agreed and another Jewish gentleman remarked, "As I entered the tent I noticed one of your helpers had a cast over his left hand. I also noticed him climbing up and down a stepladder to place large bulbs in the sockets in order to bring light into the tent. Is that man also a Christian?"

I naturally guessed that this man had also failed the Lord, but I did not hesitate to say, "As far as I know he is a Christian."

This interrogater got very annoyed and slapped his hand hard against the mantelpiece and said, "I suppose his wife is one, too?"

I did not answer him.

"Now you come with me, my dear Christian Jewish preacher, to my jewelry store and I'll show the outstanding amount in their account, and you can have your Jesus and your Christians and I will have my account-paying Jewish friends, and the God of Abraham and Isaac and Jacob."

One thing I do know without a doubt is that if we are going to mention the name of Jesus and "profess to possess the man Christ in our hearts" we had better make sure that no one can point a finger at us and accuse us of anything that is detrimental to our lives.

Two wonderful Jewish gentlemen attended some of my services. One evening they invited both my wife and me to a steak dinner. During the meal they started to tell stories of things that were happening on their staff. The stories were sickening and I told them so. They agreed that the stories were sickening and then added, "Mr. Rubenstein, these are the church-goers on my staff that do these things, and they proclaim to be Christians, reading portions of Scripture to others every chance that they have. I am sick and tired of all their Christian nonsense, and I intend throwing the whole lot out."

I felt very embarrassed for those people that had upset my good friend, and once again felt that unless we were STRONG IN THE LORD, others would always be in a position to find fault. Legitimate fault. *The way* we live speaks a lot louder than the way *we say* that we live.

A doctor friend of mine, a good member of a good church, constantly spoke to me about "keeping the Sabbath." I fully agreed with him and told him that the Sabbath be kept but that to be sure that on the following days of the week we did not do the things that were an abomination in the sight of God. I think he got the message. People are not looking for formality, they are looking for reality. Too many churches are spending too much time on programming God instead of doing what the Lord's Prayer instructed us to do:

THY WILL BE DONE. One of the greatest popes in Italy, Pope John, told the people that when the churches had to use forms of entertainment to capture the attention of people, as well as get them to come to church, "that was the first sign of spiritual decay."

When people understand that the holy Word of God has been given for "doctrine and for reproof and for correction" they will accept with open arms and an open heart.

In one of my large meetings one evening the Lord spoke to my heart and said, "Call for the sick." This I did, fully understanding that God had spoken. Hundreds of people stood before me, then the voice spoke again, "There is a cancer case here, call for it."

I asked the many people who were standing in the front if there was anybody with cancer. There was no response. I said that there was somebody who was suffering with cancer and that God wanted them to come forward. For seven minutes we waited, and that seven minutes seemed to me like seven hours. Then from the back of the church a mother led her son down the side aisle.

The boy was very thin and weak, and as he walked toward the front many others joined those that were at the front because they had seen yet another gift of God in operation.

I directed all the sick to go into a large prayer room at the side of the church, and asked for the pastor to send in helpers to pray for them as I was fatigued. He did this and I walked into that prayer room just to watch God work. Suddenly I heard somebody hissing like a snake, and when I looked it was one of the workers trying to attract my attention. She pointed to the lady she was praying with. I looked at the lady and recognized her as a woman that frequented the bars, smoked and drank very heavily and was very loose with the opposite sex.

I signaled back that she should continue to pray for her and walked away.

Not long afterwards the hissing resumed and once again the lady was beckoning me to pray for the lady that was kneeling before her. This time she came to me and said, "Brother Hymie, this lady wants you and you alone to pray for her."

I obliged in a half-hearted manner. "What do you want and what do you need?" I asked.

The lady looked up with tears running out of her eyes, and with a breath that was saturated with smoke and strong liquor said, "I want to be baptized with the Holy Ghost."

My mind instantly told me that there was no hope for a woman in that condition, but to avoid any future disputes I laid my hands on her, and as I was praying she burst forth into a glorious heavenly language.

Between my experience in the tent and my experience with that woman who had a breath full of nicotine and strong liquor I made up my mind never ever to judge or condemn another soul as long as I lived.

Lorne Fox, a popular American evangelist, was speaking at a meeting that my wife and I attended. After each meeting he would call for those in need to come to the front. Invariably hundreds would respond, and after he would pray for the hundreds each one would lay prostrate on the floor. My wife desired to have Lorne Fox pray for her. Her back had been troubling her. When Mr. Fox gave the invitation my wife joined hundreds of people at the front. This time before praying for anybody Lorne Fox walked up and down in front of the people for some time.

My wife had told me that she did not intend falling on the floor like everybody else was doing. Strangely enough the man stopped in front of my wife and said, "Lady, I perceive that you are full of pain." As he moved to lay his hands upon her my wife fell prostrate to the floor. I spoke to her about this a little later and she said that she had no idea what had happened to her. "But one thing I do know" she said, "I felt a lot better when I got up off the floor."

One day while downtown at the City Hall, I noticed that there was a cenotaph standing at the right hand side of the building. Cenotaph meant only one thing to me and I intended to use it as the one thing that it meant to me, not later but immediately. I spent the next hour there calling "sinners to repentance" and telling them that "the joy of the Lord could be their strength." The response was weak but the message was strong.

It was a few days later that I experienced some very bad, aching teeth. I knew that I would have to go and see some dentist in the city to attend to this condition.

I walked along the sidewalk looking for a place that I could see some advertisement where there was a dentist. A-cross from the City Hall there was a notice board which read: Dr. Mannie Botes, Dentist.

After locating the place I asked the receptionist if there was a possibility to get immediate help, and apologized that I had not made any previous arrangements.

"I guess we can fill you in sometime this morning," she said.

Others were called in before me, and then, as usual, when my turn came butterflies began flying in my stomach. I sat in the chair, the nurse put a white bib around my neck and the dentist came in and began examing me. He said there were five teeth that needed filling, but I told him just one was troubling me.

He suggested that I have all five teeth filled right then, and before I could answer him he filled my mouth with all kinds of tools and filled five teeth.

He then suggested that it was necessary to have my teeth cleaned and I tried to tell him that I would return at a later date to have that job done. He once again answered by filling my mouth with other appliances and began to clean.

The more he worked inside my big mouth the more my big heart decreased in size. It was the first time that I had met the man, and I knew just how expensive it was to have one tooth filled, let alone *five.* When he concluded he thanked me and I climbed out of that chair hoping that my feet and my knees would carry me.

I waited for him to write out the cost and then he called his lady assistant into the room and pointed to me and said, "Do you remember this man?"

The nurse looked at me and said that my face was familiar but she could not recall having seen me in any particular place. The dentist took her by the arm and led her to the window and pointed out the window and said, "Don't you remember this man standing right there?"

The nurse remained puzzled and then again he said, "Only a few days ago you and I stood in this window and listened to a man standing at that cenotaph preaching the Gospel of our Lord Jesus Christ."

The nurse answered with a loud, "Hallelujah, praise the Lord, now I remember!"

When I asked the dentist what I owed him he replied, Good Sir, it's not what you owe us, it's what we owe you. We thank you from the bottom of our hearts for the day you stood at the cenotaph and reminded us that there was a God that was concerned and cared and blessed His children."

I was so thrilled I felt like jumping out that third floor window and running to the cenotaph to continue where I had left off the last time.

The dentist invited me to his home one evening and my wife and I sat in a beautiful living room talking to him about "the way, the truth and the life." Mrs. Botes said that she did not understand how people could possibly have such faith in God by not having a steady job, nor a steady income.

I replied that money could not buy the experiences and the blessings that God gives those who serve Him in spirit and in truth. I related the story about a man that they were well acquainted with that I forbade to walk out of my service one night before I had prayed with him, and how that man had handed me a revolver after I had prayed with him. Piet Nel had told me that if I had not prayed with him that night that he was going to shoot and kill a man that he had hated for years.

Chapter Fourteen
A Great Big Wonderful God

My own eyes had seen the supernatural power of the supernatural God, but one thing I was to learn was that "the ways of God are past finding out."

I could not understand that during a terrible time of gall trouble, pain and suffering that I could not receive my healing. Many times in the healing line I would pray for hundreds of people who had the same complaint that I had—gall bladder trouble. Time and again one of those people would return glorifying God for the perfect way that He had healed from this ailment.

One time I lay on a church floor for a day and a night calling to God to hear me and heal me of this trouble. He heard me but He did not heal me.

There were days during a revival that I would spend the whole day in bed in pain and agony and ten minutes prior to the service I would leave the house in time to walk to the pulpit and deliver the message. Directly after closing in prayer I would rush back to my bed and once again lay in pain and agony. I lived for months on pound cake and milk.

Whatever strength I had was only spiritual, but nothing physical. I was eventually obliged to visit a doctor in Toledo, Ohio, who had known about me and who had known about my faith in God.

He showed me the x-ray and I could see that big black stones had lodged in the gall. The doctor said, "Hymie, except you have have these removed shortly, I can assure you that you will be removed permanently."

To the amazement of many of my friends I had my gall bladder removed.

The doctor found that peritonitis had set in and that gangrene would have followed, and would likely have killed me. I was aware that in spite of the many sarcastic remarks that many professing Christians made about my operation, I continued to do more for God without my gall bladder than they would ever do for God in their lives with their gall bladder.

The young man who dashed to my home one day and demanded that I immediately pray for him was surprised when I refused to.

"That is what you are here for," he demanded. "Pray for me, I need prayer."

I asked him to simmer down a bit and to tell me his troubles.

He explained he had lost his job, that his wife had lost her job, that his children were all sick in bed, and that they were finding it difficult "to make ends meet." Once again he said, "Come on, man, pray for us."

I looked at the man and said, "I refuse to pray for you, but I want to give you some good advice."

He told me that he had been sick and tired of being given "good advice" and that he wanted prayer.

I said, "Young man, if you will pay your tithe you will find that God will open the windows of heaven for you, and you will be well, and your family will be well, and everything will be wonderful for you."

The man's eyes practically popped out of his head.

"How on earth do you know that I refuse to pay my tithe?" he asked.

I had felt in the spirit that this was his shortcoming, and the sooner he patched up that little bit of patchwork great things would happen in his life.

After he had faithfully promised that he would take my advice, I prayed and told God that there was now a new tither in the business.

I visited a church a few months later and was so delighted to see that the choir leader was the new tither with happiness bubbling, bubbling, bubbling over in his soul. The pastor told what a blessing this young man was to the church. I asked him a little question and he replied, "Yes, Sir, he's one of the most faithful tithers in my church."

Many thousands of others have found the beauty of serving God and receiving abundant blessings from Him through my encouraging them to "give to Caesar what is due unto Caesar, and never to forget to give God what is due unto God, and to see if He would not open the windows of heaven for them."

The place to pay tithe is "in the storehouse" and that storehouse is the church where you are being fed. We could not enjoy food at McDonalds and then go to the Elias Big Boy Restaurant and pay them for the food received from McDonalds! God wants us to donate much to His work that His work might proceed unhindered. Some have felt that they should pay their tithe where *they* thought they should pay it, but if they were to die they could not get the man or the woman whose ministry they loved but lived thousands of miles away to come and bury them, or come and pray for them in their needs.

My wife and I have been taught from the very commencement of our Christian life, "pay your tithe and give with a cheerful heart and God will give to you good measure, shaken together, pressed down and running over."

The Prophet Joel mentioned the fact that there shall be visions. There are two kinds of visions—the genuine vision that comes from God, and the artificial vision that comes from overeating.

In my lifetime I've been blessed with numerous visions.

The one I received in the city of Bethlehem where I saw the Master nailed to an old rugged cross—the second vision that I saw was during a pastor's seminar. After a few days of praying and fasting the pastors stood in a large circle to close the meeting with prayer. I noticed two hands assisting a pastor who was finding it very difficult to cut the sheaves that he might bring them in. The two hands were nail-scarred and the road that I could see let me know whose hands they were. And with these hands the pastor was relieved of the sickle that he seemed to be using incorrectly, and the sickle now began to cut into the harvest with great results. I told the vision to the pastors and there was much rejoicing.

The following year after the pastors had spent a few days in prayer and fasting we once again stood in the circle to close with prayer. This time I noticed a beautiful golden faucet standing in the center of the prayer group and the handle was a bright silver. I had never seen such a beautiful type of gold or silver but there was no water running out of the faucet. Suddenly a nail-pierced hand appeared once again, and as the nail-pierced hand began to turn the silver handle on the faucet a great stream of water came forth. Pastors were once again elated.

I was praying one morning when suddenly I beheld a large unused gold mine. There was a large lid over the entrance to the gold mine so that nobody could enter. It surprised me with the simple way that I bent over and reached out and lifted the lid away from the entrance. Suddenly a multitude of people of every race, color and creed rushed into the gold mine, each one carrying an empty bucket. As they emerged from the mine I noticed that everyone of them had a bucket filled with gold nuggest. They were rejoicing and singing and dancing.

On another occasion during prayer I noticed a large river bed that was dry. I looked up into the hills to the mouth of that river bed and it appeared that it had been dry for many long years. Suddenly somebody placed my books on the hill by the mouth of the river and a deluge of water came gushing out like a great thick, wide, powerful waterfall. I knew by these visions that God had spoken to my heart, and "He that hath promised shall perform." Thousands of thirsty people began drinking again.

Mr. Gordon Outlaw was driving me to a service one evening in Trenton, Michigan. He told me that he had arranged for me to pray for a director of a radio station at seven o'clock sharp. We pulled up at a telephone booth at the exact time, and after dialing his number I prayed fervently for God to heal him in the mighty name of Jesus. Simultaneously the power of Almighty God hit both the director and me. By the shouting and rejoicing I heard coming from the other end of the line, I had very little doubt that the Great Physician had answered that phone call. I joined in the merriment and began rejoicing and jumping in the telephone booth. Gordon knew that something had taken place and also joined the celebration.

I don't know how that behavior appeared or appealed to the passersby but that evening I knew that there were two men in the whole wide world who had "their heads anointed with oil and their cups running over."

One of my friends was having much difficulty in persuading a farmer that it was necessary to be submerged in water baptism. For months he would go to the farm once a week impressed that the Lord would have him speak to the man about nothing but water baptism.

One particular day he made up his mind that this would be his final call. "I have other important things to attend to," he told himself.

That morning as he sat in the kitchen once more explaining to the farmer what he had explained so many times before, he concluded by saying, "Well, my friend, I have done all I know how to do, and I believe that God has done the same, so I will no longer be visiting you."

The farmer sprang out of his seat like a coil that had recoiled, rushed out of the kitchen, down the stairs and rushed along the dusty trail screaming, "Baptize me, baptize me."

My friend chased him hoping to stop him and arrange for a formal baptismal service in the church, but that farmer jumped into the dam, clothes and all, followed by the pastor, who jumped in clothes and all, and that day another soul was buried in the waters of baptism.

The pastor always took delight in telling us that "when God moves no man stoppeth."

He also used to delight in telling us how he worked on the railway and early one morning he was awakened by a tapping on the window of his room. He spotted a bird tapping repeatedly on the window. He got up and chased the bird away, and as he returned to the bed to sleep the tapping resumed. Two and three times he chased the bird away, but it returned to tap on the window. He decided that if he would close the curtains the bird would not continue the tapping. He closed the curtains but it did not make any difference to the bird, it kept tapping away louder than ever.

The tired railway worker decided to let the bird have its fun at that window so he went into the room at the back of the house and was on the verge of falling asleep again when there was tapping on the window. That same bird had followed him. He realized that this could only be something supernatural.

Then he was aware that he had not been faithful to God, and recalled the time that God had called him into the ministry and he had refused; he felt lost and undone. He fell to his knees and repented, walked to the railway station that morning, handed in his resignation, quit working for the railway and began working for God Almighty.

The times that I have dedicated babies to the Lord have been some of my happiest moments.

Some babies have bawled in my ears and kicked, while others have wet the new suit I was wearing, but the happiness that bubbled up in my heart could not allow me to become discouraged.

I've also experienced happy times of seeing a young believer see the Holy Ghost in action, by baptizing people and seeing them speak with other tongues. The happiness I have had to see faces of bitterness change to faces of sweetness. All the money in the world could never bring that joy and peace and love as those experiences.

Many times I would sit in a first grade baby Sunday school class and find more happiness there than in any other class in the church. I would recall that Jesus had said, "Except we become as babes we shall not see the kingdom of God."

I've overflowed with happiness to see people make restitution in their churches. When one would go to the other and tell them of the wrong that they had said about them and ask forgiveness. God would confirm that action by some of the greatest blessings that people had ever experienced.

I have always encouraged my congregations to "pray for the peace of Jerusalem."

Apart from my Jewish friends who once visited me in a tent meeting, I had fourteen come to a church where I was conducting services. They had come as they said, "to be healed by an *unknown* power." I told them that that power might be *unknown* to them, but I knew the *unknown* power not to be *unknown.*

I prayed for fourteen Jewish people in the name of Jesus that night, and fourteen Jewish people received a touch from their Messiah and were instantly healed. I had no sooner completed praying for the first man who had been a bad asthma sufferer when he jumped around banging his chest and breathing deeply and shouting, "Yes, I am healed, look how I breathe, I am healed!"

This naturally built great faith in the hearts of the remaining thirteen Jewish people, and they were likewise touched by the hand of the Master and healed.

On one occasion the choir was closing the service singing, "I'd rather have Jesus" when two Jewish ladies came into the church, ran down the center aisle, jumped on the platform and stood in the choir. At first it did seem funny to see everybody standing there in full dress regalia and these two women without.

I walked over to the ladies and asked them whether they intended joining the choir. They laughed and said, "No, we don't believe like you people believe but we have come along to be healed."

I prayed for them and anointed them with oil according to the Word of God. Mrs. Segal became one of my best advertisements and invited many of her Jewish friends to attend church if they needed healing.

During an altar call one Sunday morning as I prayed for many people I noticed a lady at the back desperately reaching forward to be touched. I touched her, and like the others she partook of the Lord's supper. After the conclusion of the meeting I went to relax in the prayer room when that lady came to me and said in Jewish, "Don't you remember me, Hymie?" I did not recognize the lady.

"I am your auntie Mickey Marks," she said.

I felt great joy when I saw members of my own family coming to Christ, although no immediate member of my family openly admitted receiving Jesus into their hearts at that time.

I noticed a couple in the Assembly of God church in St. Johns, Michigan, one evening ridiculing practically everything I was saying. Usually I would stop and ask for respect in the house of God, but that evening I did not.

After the service the pastor told me that there were a couple of infuriated people waiting for me in his office. I walked into the office and found that the couple who were waiting for me were the same couple that were acting idiotically in the church.

"Are you trying to bring an anti-semitic movement in this country?" they asked. They had been sent there to represent a group that had taken a very bad view of what I had been doing in that area.

I explained that I had taken a very bad view of what *they* had been doing in the area and rebuked them for their most indecent and disrespectful behavior in the house of God. And that respectable Jewish persons would never have shown disrespect for anybody's belief and church, that I knew the Jewish people to be members of a noble race and the most charming, intelligent and wonderful crowd of people that one could ever desire to associate with. "Your behavior is far from that," I assured them.

The couple stood there for a long time. Whatever they intended saying to me, or doing to me, they had forgotten.

I continued, that to be Jewish was something to be proud of. Both Peter and Paul, the disciples of Jesus Christ, were never ashamed to let the world know that they were Jews. I suggested that we should hold hands and ask God to guide us, and to keep "our tongues from evil and our mouths that they might speak no guile."

The man looked very sheepishly at his wife and said, "You know, Rachel, I have heard of many Jewish people being converted in these days."

I was quite sure he was a most likely candidate that night—until his wife rebuked him and said, "Don't be stupid Solly. Let's get out of here."

I held their hands tightly and prayed and felt that my Friend was near at hand. I noticed tears streaming down their faces.

They left the church that night with an entirely different spirit.

Chapter Fifteen
Thank You, My Lovely Jesus

One evening on my way to hold a service my heart just kept bubbling over with joy. I thought about the way God had so mercifully delivered me out of unhappiness and placed a song in my heart. I began to count my blessings one by one. I persuaded myself that it was worth everything to serve God.

I realized I wasn't in jail. I wasn't in a hospital or the mental institution, and above all I wasn't in the place called hell.

I was whistling loudly as I turned in to a restaurant that the pastor and his assistant frequented. As usual, they were sitting there waiting for me.

A young woman sat at a table at the entrance. As I looked at her she smiled and winked at me. I looked at her again and she winked at me for the second time. She motioned to the chair with her hand, indicating that she wanted me to join her.

I ignored her and joined my two friends.

We discussed the future programs for the services, as well as the moving of God's Spirit that we had witnessed night after night. I began thinking about the many people who were not attending the meetings. I thought about their chances of missing eternal life.

One of them was sitting at the table at the entrance of the very place that I was in!

I stood up and excused myself, "Gentlemen, kindly excuse me," I said, "but I have a very pressing engagement to keep with a woman who is not only going to become a very good friend of mine, but also my sister." They were surprised to see me join the winker who had signaled me to join her.

As I sat down at the table she assured me that she "could give me the time of my life." She laughed aloud as I assured her that I could do likewise and "give her the time of her life."

She got very childish and excited for a moment, but when I said, "Have you ever tried to let Jesus Christ of Nazareth come into your heart and give you the time of your life," she turned pale and tongue-tied at the same time.

I fed her with a few scriptures, making sure that I would not give her indigestion. I invited her to the tent services. Tears began welling up in her eyes as she said, "I will come."

What a shame she didn't.

Time and again people would promise me that they would attend my services and fail to keep their promises. The excuses that they would offer when I would catch them the second time around were at times an insult to man's intelligence.

When I would consider what they were missing my heart would break. To me it seemed to be so very easy, and to them it appeared to be a mighty mountain that stood in the way.

The first Sunday after my testimony a Frenchman viciously grabbed me by my coat as I entered the church. He pulled me into a small room under the stairway and banged the door behind him. "Please, get me back to God. Please get me back to God," he screamed.

I asked him how he ever got away from God.

"Brother Hymie," he said, "I used to thoroughly enjoy holding open-air services in Paris, France, every Saturday morning. I would always have my little box with me to stand on, and the results were most encouraging.

"One morning as I was preaching a firey message my pastor came and commanded me to step off the box and quit. At first I thought he was joking, but he told me that he had not given me permission to hold open-air services and pushed me off the little box very roughly. For a moment I stood there unbelieving. I was dumbfounded and walked away not fully comprehending what had taken place. I felt an arm slip through mine and smelled a beautiful scent inside my nostrils. A very pretty young girl squeezed my arm," he said.

"My dear lovely French preacher man, don't be discouraged at what has happened to you. Come home with me and I will take extra good care of you," the girl suggested.

The Frenchman explained that in his defeated condition he accepted the invitation without considering the fact that it was annoying to God.

"Brother Hymie, I stayed with that girl for nine solid months. We lived like husband and wife and many times I had said to her that we should be married and discontinue living the way we were, and told her that God did not approve of it.

"One day that girl ran into the apartment and demanded me to pack up and leave instantly as the ship that her husband was working on was docking shorly."

In his backslidden condition the Frenchman looked up to God and sought help. He felt that the Spirit of the Lord had forsaken him and for years he had failed to feel the touch of God upon his life once more.

I explained that I would see him after the service as it was time for me to address the large audience that had gathered, but he blocked my way and stood in front of the door and said with tears streaming down his face, "Sir, I love you as a servant of the Lord, but tonight you'll have to kill me before I will permit you to walk out of here without getting my Jesus to give me the blessed assurance that I am His and that He has forgiven me and that He is mine."

I held his face in my hands and in a few seconds Jesus let him know that he was His.

The man stepped aside from the door and fell on the floor, and as I closed the door all I could hear him continue to say was, "Thank you, my lovely Jesus."

As usual, that night was once again truly blessed because one who had strayed away from the fold had found that the Good Shepherd had left the ninety and nine and came and found him and returned him again to the flock. Many others who had wearied along the road, many others who had been sidetracked, many others who had been deceived, and many others who had lost a battle or two once again found themselves as "soldiers of the King marching as to war, with the cross of Jesus going on before."

I left that area with much foreboding and trusted that if I did not meet those soldiers of the King down here on this old earth I would one day meet them "walking on the streets of gold with Jesus who is the light."

As I look back upon the thousands that I have helped and blessed and guided out of the darkness into His wonderful light, I say, "Hallelujah!"

To see the reality of God, and to watch Him move by His Spirit is something that words cannot explain.

At no time during my years of dedicated service have I seen denominational and traditional barriers razed, as today. Like the woman whom Jesus met at the well in Samaria, the whole wide world is crying out spiritually, "Sir, give me this water that I thirst not."

As I preach "Christ and Christ crucified" doors have been opened to me in places where they were once tightly shut.

I find hungry hearts yearning for green pastures and still waters. So many have become weary of receiving the same "news report" from the pulpit as from the TV and radio. I feed them "God's News" for which there is no substitute.

As the Saviour saves, heals, sanctifies, satisfies and confirms His Word with signs following, I see churches (that allow "Thy will be done") having bigger attendances, buying more buses and having to either expand or rebuild.

The Full Gospel Businessmen (an organization comprising mainly of laymen) are sending witnesses around the world. I was the original speaker for this group in my own hometown in Lansing, Michigan. Thirteen people attended. Today the attendance is six hundred.

Soon the time of the Gentiles will be fulfilled.

Jewish people will be coming out of the darkness into His wonderful light. I continue to bless them that I might be blessed. I pray for the peace of Jerusalem that I may prosper. Jesus (Messiah Yeshua) himself said, "First to the Jew."

As God continues to open the eyes of the blind, they cannot fail to see that the prophecy of Joel the prophet is coming forth "full speed." God is pouring out His Spirit upon all flesh regardless of sex, race, creed or color. Regardless of denomination or tradition. It is a great big glorious day and time to be alive. God is in heaven and He is very much in "full control."

To the Reader

So many experiences I have related to the readers of this book, and yet not by far have they been exhausted.

The great thing that has come to be in my mind while writing this book was the blessed assurance that someone, somewhere would dedicate or rededicate their lives to the Lamb of God, who alone bringeth joy into the hearts of His children. "Who forgiveth all thine iniquities; who healeth all thy diseases; who redeemeth thy life from destruction; who crowneth thee with lovingkindness and tender mercies; who satisfieth thy mouth with good things" (Psalm 103:3-5).

You have read many stories in this book and only God "who is a discerner of the thoughts and knows the intents of the heart" is aware of your opinions and findings.

My initial intention in writing this book is that every reader "without fail" shall experience, either for the first time or once again, the beautiful touch of God.

By making your request or requirement known to Him right now, I believe with nothing wavering that a new thing will most undoubtedly take place in your life.

I respectfully ask you to hold this book lightly in your hands and pray this prayer aloud—most earnestly and most sincerely:

My dear and most wonderful, good, kind and understanding God, I know that You are the great creator of heaven and earth. I know that I am part of your creation.

I have read this book. I am sure that the author is both a chosen vessel unto You, and also a faithful servant. I believe he has done his best to increase my faith and trust and belief in You.

I also believe that your Son Jesus Christ of Nazareth

from Galilee shed His blood on Calvary, and that by his stripes I am healed—body, soul and spirit.

I do not hesitate to right now accept Him as my Lord, my Saviour and Redeemer.

Therefore, wonderful Father which art in heaven, without any reservation or doubt or fear I now call upon You in the name of the only begotten Son, Jesus the Christ of Nazareth.

I repent of all my sins and iniquities. I know that I am a sinner, but I know that the blood of Jesus cleanses from all sin. Please cleanse me. Make me pure and perfect and holy in your sight that I too may be a chosen vessel unto You. Be merciful to me and cause your face to shine upon me.

Send me and use me that others might be set free from this sin-sick world. I will serve You with all my heart, all my mind and all my strength. Allow me to become your hand extended, reaching out for the oppressed.

Yes, God, make me a blessing and a help to the multitudes who are wandering in sin, sickness and darkness.

Heavenly Father, I ask that You deliver me out of the miry clay, and place my feet on the King's highway that I in turn might help the needy, feed the hungry and give drink to the thirsty. Endue me with power from on high.

I know now dear God, that this prayer has been answered. I give You and You alone all the praise, all the honor, all the glory and all the thanks.

In the name of Jesus the Christ of Nazareth, I say, Amen and Amen."

NEW TAPES

HR1500- Hymie's Testimony

HR1501- When the Heart Cries

HR1502- Your Wall of Jericho

HR1503- God's Sheep Market

HR1504- Look on Us

HR1505- Count Your Blessings

HR1506- What Price Jesus

HR1507- Unclogging Your Well

HR1508- Kill Yourself a Giant

HR1509- The Whole Thing

HR1510- Bubbling Bubbling Over

HR1511- Whove! Whove! Whove!

HR1512- Isaacs are Pests

HR1513- Own an Oil Well & Bakery

HR1514- Three Jewish Rabbis

HR1515- God's Bigger than Big

HR1516- I also Touched His Garment
(Mrs. Elaine Rubenstein)

PRICE FOR CASSETTES - $3.00 each

BOOKS

It's Getting Gooder and Gooder (Hymie's Life Story) $2.95

Completely Completed (Hymie's Salvation) $1.00

USE THIS ORDER FORM

QUAN.	DESCRIPTION & NUMBER	COST EA	TOTAL
		TOTAL	

Contact the Author for speaking engagements at:
TEMPLE TAPES & BOOKS
P. O. Box 1372, Lansing, Mich. 48901
517-351-9243